The Vietnam Conflict, 1945–75

By Alex Kerr

Edited by Liberal Publishing House

Complete Book: First Edition

'Those who fail to learn from History, are forced to repeat it.'

The last message to Washington from Saigon in 1975, from CIA Chief Thomas Polgar.

Preface:

This book intends to give as much information as possible about the history of warfare and to relate it to the IGCSE Edexcel exam board.

Alex Kerr has been teaching History and Politics for ten years. He is a graduate of Oxford Brookes University and has completed a PGCE at The Institute of Education, London as well as recently completing courses at the Johann Cruyff Institute, Barcelona.

The book will cover:

The first Indochina war

The second Indochina war, also known as the Vietnam Conflict or the Vietnam War.

This is an investigation study, so key aspects need to be learnt.

1.   The struggle against France for independence, 1945–54

2.   US policy and intervention, 1954–64

3.   Confrontation in the Vietnam War, escalation 1964–68

4.   Nixon and Ford's policies: Vietnamisation, peace & Communist victory, 1969–75

5.   The impact of conflict on civilians in Vietnam & attitudes in the USA

The exam paper is divided into three questions:

It is also divided into three question types:

(a): Wants the student to describe two key features of events or policies that took place during the Vietnam Conflict.

(b): How far does Source A support the evidence of Source B

(c): This question requires you to answer the question using all three sources and you must use all three sources and some of your own knowledge to gain full marks.

Coming Soon

There will be a supplemental book to this one, with ideas and questions on how to approach the exam paper.

Contents:

When you think of Vietnam, what do you think of?

Where is the country?

What is the significance of the country today?

What is the political background?

Well, a lot of it is connected to the Vietnam Conflict or War, which occurred from 1945 to 1975. Yet, for the Vietnamese, this was a war that had been going back even further. They were occupied by the Japanese during WW2 and before that, they were occupied by the French. The French had been operating in the area from around the 1600s, they had slowly but surely taken over the country and established a government and Catholicism as a religion in the area. For the Vietnamese, the war against a foreign army was nothing new.

Tour guide getting into one of the old Viet Cong tunnels.

Coalition: group of countries fighting together.

Guerrilla: a type of war, including tactics such as hit and run. Small groups, rather than large armies, attack when the enemy is weak.

Sabotage: destroying something, e.g., power lines, pipelines.

Terrain: the land, e.g. mountains, jungle, forest, etc.

Morale: the enthusiasm of people.

Booby traps: traps for soldiers (fall into a spiked pit, etc.) often set-off by a wire.

Search and destroy: tactic used by the US in Vietnam. Helicopters bring in soldiers, they attack a specific area such as a village, then leave.

Rolling Thunder: name given to the bombing of North Vietnam by US Stealth aircraft planes that avoid being seen by radar.

Napalm: a petrol-based chemical used to kill people.

Colonialism: the idea of invading a country and putting it under the invading army's control.

Containment: the American idea of stopping the spread of communism.

Domino Theory: the idea that if one country becomes communist, other nearby countries would become communist as well.

United Nations: an organisation where nations from around the world can meet, debate and work on diplomacy to resolve conflict.

Capitalism: the idea of goods and services being exchanged for money, and a hierarchical society is acceptable.

Democracy: Greek for, "the rule of people," or "people power": the idea that people vote for other people to represent their views.

Insurgent: a person who comes into a country to cause military or political disruption to its government.

Communism: the belief and political theory that all people should be equal in society, that there should be no government, no money, no private property, a 3-day working week and that people should be provided with what they need.

Conscription/draft: people being forced to join the nation's military.

ARVN: The Army of the Republic of Vietnam, created by the Americans and the Diem government.

CIA: Central Intelligence Agency is an American intelligence service, with the aim of gathering, processing and analysing information from around the world.

Cadre: trained and dedicated Communist Party workers who organised resistance in South Vietnam's countryside and cities.

NVA: The North Vietnamese Army was founded by Ho Chi Minh in 1944, to attack the Japanese and then South Vietnam and America.

NLF: National Liberation Front was created under Le Duan and his supporters in 1960. Their aim was to get rid of the Southern Government of Vietnam and the foreigners that supported him.

PLF: Peoples Liberation Armed Forces were the military side of the N.L.F and would become known as the Viet Cong.

Viet Cong: A communist political organization in South Vietnam, who used guerrilla tactics.

Hard Hats: Construction workers who supported the Vietnam War and soldiers.

Congress: A building that contains the House of Representatives and the Senate.

House of representatives: Representatives are elected by people to represent their views to government. The representatives are called congresswomen or congressman and they are elected from a small than a state local area. Each state gets a different number of representative based on their population size.

Senate: Representatives elected by people. The representatives are called Senators and represent a specific state.

Ho Chi Minh:

He adopted 70 different names in his lifetime. The final name means 'enlightened one.' Born in 1890, he was exiled and lived in Paris, London, where he discovered Lenin and Communism, then went to Moscow for Soviet training. He returned to China, developed a pro-Vietnamese Communist group. He returned in 1941 and created the Viet Minh.

Le Duc Tho:

A North Vietnamese representative at secret negotiations with the United States and Henry Kissinger. He was a revolutionary veteran with 40 years' experience. He was awarded the Noble Peace Prize in 1973 for his efforts in bringing peace between North Vietnam and America.

General Gaip:

General of the North Vietnam Armies, who was originally a French teacher. He converted to communism after the French beat his wife to death in prison.

Le Duan:

Son of a carpenter, he founded the Indochinese Communist Party. Survived ten years in a French prison. He gained influence in the North Vietnamese politburo and began to change its policy. He argued that everything should be done to support the South Vietnamese, which was going against Ho Chi Minh's cautionary policy, to reunify the country. This policy encouraged North Vietnamese to move south along the Ho Chi Minh trail.

Ngo Dinh Diem:

A Catholic and Confucian, he had travelled abroad seeking support for his version of democracy. He hated the French and the Communists. He had suffered because of the Communists, who had imprisoned him and buried alive his eldest brother and nephew. Diem was able to gain power in South Vietnam through rigged voting.

Trần Lệ Xuân/Madam Nhu:

Wife of Ngo Dinh Nhu, considered to be a significant power in the South Vietnamese Diem regime, continually made inflammatory comments throughout the regime. She died in 2011.

Ngo Dinh Nhu:

The brother of Diem oversaw the South Vietnamese government and the secret police of South Vietnam. He helped his brother gain power of South Vietnam in 1955. He died in 1963 after a South Vietnamese military coup.

General de Lattre:

Commander of the French armies in Vietnam from 1950-1951. Born in 1889 and died in 1962. He oversaw Dien Bien Phu but was no longer in charge before its collapse.

President Truman:

President of the United States from 1945–1953, strong anti-communist views. He initiated the events in Vietnam with support for the French in holding the colony.

President Eisenhower:

President of the United States from 1953 to 1961. He continued the major aid to the French and the South Vietnam government. He led the formation of the Southeast Asia Treaty Organization. It was an alliance with Britain, France, New Zealand and Australia, with the aim of defending Vietnam and stopping communism.

President Kennedy:

President of the United States from 1961 to 1963. He continued the major aid to the South Vietnam government. Including increasing military advisors and commandos.

President Johnson:

President of the United States from 1963 to 1969. He became president after the assassination of President Kennedy. He led huge welfare programmes during his presidency as well as significant civil rights acts. In Vietnam and foreign affairs, he had kept President Kennedy's staff.

He continues to hope that America's will to persevere can be broken. Well, he is wrong.

President Nixon:

President of the United States from 1969 to 1974. He had also been Vice-President under President Eisenhower. He caused the first peace talks to collapse before he was President. He promoted the idea of removing troops from Vietnam, yet escalated the war in Cambodia and Laos.

President Ford:

President of the United States from 1974–1977. He was President during the final days of Saigon. Attempted to get funding from Congress to support the South Vietnamese government but was unable to achieve this.

Robert McNamara:

He was United States Secretary of Defence from 1961–1968. He had aimed at controlling and organising the war through statistics.

Henry Kissinger:

He was key to the peace agreements succeeding between the Americans and North Vietnamese, allowing the Americans to withdraw from South Vietnam. He was awarded the Noble Peace Prize in 1973. However, in 1975 after the fall of Saigon, Kissinger tried to take the award back.

General Westmoreland:

Commander of the Vietnam War from 1964–1968 and followed a similar belief to Robert McNamara: that the war was to be won through statistics and that the real aim was to kill more people than the North Vietnamese could kill.

13

1945

Ho Chi Minh creates a Provisional Government

Ho declares Vietnam independent

Britain lands troops in Saigon,

Britain returns authority to France

First American dies in Vietnam

1946

France and Viet Minh reach agreements

Agreements between France and Vietminh Breakdown

Indochina War starts

1947

Vietminh move north of Hanoi

1950

China and the Soviet Union (Russia today) offer weapons to Viet Minh

The US pledges $15M in aid to France

1953

France grants Laos independence

Viet Minh troops enter into Laos

1954

Battle of Dien Bien Phu starts

Eisenhower discusses "Domino Theory" in regards to Southeast Asia

France defeated at Dien Bien Phu

Geneva Convention begins

Geneva Convention Agreements announced

> - Vietnam Split along the 17th parallel
> - Laos officially created
> - Cambodia officially created
> - France agrees to leave Vietnam

1955

President of South Vietnam, Diem rejects the Geneva Accords and refuses to participate in Elections or Referendum for a united Vietnam.

China and Soviet Union pledge further financial support to North Vietnam.

1956

France leaves Vietnam

The US begins training South Vietnamese Troops

Diem holds elections in South Vietnam

1957

Communists begin to come into South Vietnam. (Also known as Insurgency)

Saigon suffers from terrorist bombings from Viet Minh.

1958

National Liberation Front created.

1959

Ho Chi Minh Trail starts to have weapons and supplies coming down it to support South Vietnamese Communists.

US Servicemen are killed in a guerrilla attack

President Diem begins crackdown of communists, Buddhists, gangs and opposition.

1960

North Vietnam starts military conscription

John F. Kennedy is elected President of the United States.

President Diem survived first coup attempt.

South Vietnamese created their own Communist political and military group known as the Viet Cong.

Y.A.F created.

1961

Vice President of the United States Johnson visits Saigon.

Number of military advisors increased.

Agent Orange first used

1962

US Military begins to use Agent Orange.

South Vietnam's Presidential Palace bombed in another coup attempt.

Strategic Hamlet Programme started.

1963

President Kennedy assassinated in Dallas; Lyndon Johnson becomes president.

Buddhists protest Diem government by burning themselves and public demonstrations.

President Diem and his brother Nhu are overthrown and murdered. Nhu's wife escapes as she is in the U.S.

1964

General Nguyen Khanh Seizes Power in Saigon.

Gulf of Tonkin Incidents.

President Johnson sends 20,000 advisors.

Gulf of Tonkin resolution passed by Congress.

16

1965

Operation "Rolling Thunder" started.

First American combat troops arrive at Danang.

US Troop Levels Top 200,000.

Anti-war "Teach-In" protests broadcast to American Universities.

S.D.S. has 3000 members.

1966

B-52s bombers bomb North Vietnam for the first time

South Vietnam Government troops take the cities of Hue and Danang

President Johnson meets with leaders of South Vietnamese

Veterans stage an Anti-War rally in Washington D.C.

1967

Dr Martin Luther King Speaks Out Against War

Robert McNamara states that the bombing is ineffective

Largest Pro-War rally held in New York.

1968

January

North Vietnam launches Tet Offensive .

Walter Cronkite announces Vietnam cannot be won.

February

General Westmoreland requests 206,000 more troops.

My Lai Massacre.

March

President Johnson announces he won't run for a second term as president.

April

Dr King assassinated in Memphis.

1968

May

Paris Peace Talks begin.

August

Protests at the Democratic Convention in Chicago

September

NSCVV created.

November

Richard Nixon elected President

1969

Nixon begins the secret bombing of Cambodia and Ho Chi Minh trail.

"Vietnamization" started; American troops start to be withdrawn.

Ho Chi Minh dies at the age of 79.

News of My Lai Massacre reaches the U.S.

Massive Anti-war Demonstration in Washington D.C.

Draft system becomes a lottery.

1970

Kent State Incident.

Henry Kissinger & Le Duc start secret talks.

The number of US troops reduced to 280,000.

24% of South Vietnam had been sprayed with defoliant.

U.S. invaded Cambodia.

Hard Hats (Construction workers.) riot takes place in New York.

1971

Lt. Calley who was involved in the My Lai Massacre is convicted of Murder.

The Pentagon Papers are published.

Nixon announces he will visit China.

ARVN invades Laos and fails.

1972

Nixon reduces the number of troops by 70,000

B-52s bomb Hanoi and Haiphong

The criminals breaking into the Watergate Hotel discovered and arrested

Kissinger announces "Peace Is At Hand"

Nixon wins a second term as President

North Vietnam invades South Vietnam and is pushed back by US and ARVN forces.

1973

Only 150 marines left in South Vietnam in January.

A cease-fire is signed in Paris.

The United States announces that conscription/the draft has stopped.

Last American troops leave Vietnam.

Kissinger and Le Duc Tho both win the Noble Peace Prize.

1974

President of South Vietnam, Thieu, announces the renewal of War

Communists take Mekong Delta Territory, which is north of Saigon

Nixon resigns as President

1975

The city of Hue captured by Communists

Ford announces the Vietnam War as "Finished"

Last Vietnam based American troops are killed

 Last Americans evacuate as Saigon Falls to Communists

Definition of Guerrilla Warfare:

North Vietnam General Giap stated that his Viet Cong guerrillas were:

"Everywhere and nowhere."

Guerrilla warfare can be replicated anywhere there is cover and where the advantages of cover cannot be used by a more significant and/or conventional force.

Leaders like China's Communist leader Mao Zedong and North Vietnamese Leader Ho Chi Minh both used guerrilla warfare, giving it a base, which served as a model for similar strategies elsewhere, such as Al Qaeda in Afghanistan.

Mao Zedong summarised basic guerrilla tactics as:

"The enemy advances, we retreat; the enemy camps, we harass; the enemy tires, we attack; the enemy retreats, we pursue."

Communist leaders like Mao Zedong and North Vietnamese Ho Chi Minh both employed guerrilla warfare in the style of 'The Art of War.'

Chapter 1

The struggle against France for independence, 1945–54

The origins of the First Indochina War, especially the aims of the Vietminh.

The origins of the First Indochina War arguably started all the way back in the 1600s with the French starting to occupy Vietnam. However, we do not need to go as far back as that. What we need to know is that the French began fully occupying the country in the 1800s until 1940. In September 1940 the Japanese invaded Vietnam, which was part of World War Two. The Japanese were successful and installed a puppet government, who were French, and they ruled on Japan's behalf. In 1941, a Vietnamese man by the name of Ho Chi Minh returned to Vietnam and formed an organisation that was to become very important in Vietnam's bid for independence. They were called the Viet Nam Doc Lap Dong Minh Hoi (League for the Independence of Vietnam), better known as the Việt Minh. Inside schools, nationalism was starting to be taught. These ideas, and the maltreatment by the French who considered the Vietnamese to be inferior caused further hatred and resentment, fuelling the cause to remove the French.

The Viet Minh were supplied by the USA to begin a campaign against the Japanese. Ho Chi Minh praised the Americans as a champion of democracy and believed that they would help end colonial rule, even calling the Viet Minh the Viet-American Army. By August of 1945, the Japanese had surrendered. Ho and the Viet Minh announced their liberation from the French, the Japanese and that they were an independent country. He even used the first lines of the American Declaration of Independence to make his announcement.

Ho Chi Minh on the far right, wearing shorts. General Giap on the left.

"We hold the truth that all men are created equal, that they are endowed by their Creator with certain unalienable rights, among them life, liberty and the pursuit of happiness."

Even with the liberation and this fantastic declaration, the Vietnamese were still not free and were having to discuss terms with the French who were reluctant to let go of their conquered lands in Asia. The country was split in to two separate zones of North and South. The North was to be run by the Viet Minh and the South was to be run by British colonial troops.

The French, under President Charles De Gaulle, had wanted to keep and secure their Empire. The French had come to blows with the Chinese government. They had attempted to stay in China and reclaim old territories such as Shanghai. The Leader of China, Chiang Kai-shek, threatened war if they did not leave. In September 1945, fighting between the French and the Viet Minh in the south of Vietnam, in Saigon, had already started. Violence in and around Saigon soon escalated. The first American died in September 1945. Ironically, he was attempting to get the British and French to leave Vietnam when he was mistaken for a French officer and killed by Viet Minh troops. A week later French troops entered Saigon and quickly established control of the city.

This resulted in a meeting at the city of Haiphong, between the French and the Viet Minh.

The relations broke down over taxes in the ports and fighting ensued, with the French Navy bombarding the city and killing over 6,000 civilians. The Viet Minh retreated but soon returned under General Võ Nguyên Giáp with 30,000 troops. The Viet Minh were not successful, could not withstand the French firepower and were unable to take the city. The fighting also broke out in the city of Hanoi, where Ho Chi Minh was based. He left the city and began a guerrilla war campaign up in the mountains.

24

The Viet Minh led by General Giap and Ho Chi Minh refused to meet the French in open combat. They retreated into the hills Tan Trao deep in the hills of Tuyên Quang Province and would not meet the French head to head.

This is linked to the quote said by Mao Zedong earlier:

"The enemy advances, we retreat; the enemy camps, we harass; the enemy tires, we attack; the enemy retreats, we pursue."

Later in 1947, the French launched Operation Lea to take out the Việt Minh communications centre at Bắc Kạn. The French claimed to have killed 9,000 Viet Minh during the operation.

With the difficulties of meeting the Viet Minh in head-to-head combat, the French approached the former emperor Bảo Đại and they wanted him to set up a new government that was pro-French in Saigon. By this point, the French government was spending double the amount of money they were receiving from the Americans in loans totalling $3 Billion. The loans were designed to support the French and help in their recovery after World War Two and to help stop communism Spreading. The spreading of communism is something that will be a reoccurring theme throughout this topic.

By 1949 Vietnam was under a new government run by Bao Dai, who was given control over all aspects of bar foreign relations and defence. This was still under control of the French. As you can imagine this was not what the Viet Minh wanted:

"Real independence, not Bảo Đại independence"

By the end of 1949, the Chinese government had changed and become communist giving the Viet Minh a huge, powerful, new ally. With this General Giap reorganised the Viet Minh armies into 5 infantry groups known as divisions and began to attack isolated French military bases along the Chinese-Vietnam border.

"The enemy advances, we retreat; the enemy camps, we harass; the enemy tires, we attack; the enemy retreats, we pursue."

In 1950, a new government under Ho Chi Minh was set up and both governments were recognised. Bao Dai's government was recognised by the USA and UK, and the Ho Chi Minh government was recognised by China and the USSR. In June of 1950, further concerns had come from the North and South of Korea, with North Korean Communists attacking the southern, democratic Korea. America became concerned with the unfolding events in Asia and how the region might become fully communist. With this, the American government became strongly opposed to the North Vietnam government.

Ho Chi Minh said about Korea in December 1953:

"This is the first time (but not the last) that the United States has suffered a major defeat.... The current American scheme is to provoke wars in order to become master of the world.... The [French] enemy's primary design is 'to use Vietnamese to fight Vietnamese and to use war to breed war.'... The United States is forcing France to become a puppet and plans to replace France at every step."

Militarily, the French were to suffer a series of significant defeats.

  ➤ In February, a French garrison at Lai Khê in Tonkin, just south of the border with China, was captured.
  ➤ In September, the town of Đông Khê was captured.
  ➤ The garrisons at Cao Bằng and That Khe were evacuated south. They were ambushed all the way, with a final defeat at the Battle of Route Coloniale 4. Out of roughly 10,000 French troops, 4,800 were killed, captured or missing and 2,000 wounded.

"The enemy advances, we retreat; the enemy camps, we harass; the enemy tires, we attack; the enemy retreats, we pursue."

This was only stopped when a new French General, Jean Marie de Lattre de Tassigny, took command a built a series of fortifications from Hanoi to the coast of Tonkin.

This was the first time that Napalm was used.

In January 1951, General Giap attempted to attack Vĩnh Yên, 20 miles north of Hanoi. He moved two divisions, totalling 20,000 men, north. However, this was a trap by the French, who met the Vietnamese head on and used artillery and machine guns to full effect. The Viet Minh suffered 6,000 deaths, 8,000 were wounded and 500 captured.

In March, Giap attempted another attack north of Haipong. This also resulted in a defeat with between 500-3000 Viet Minh killed.

In May, Giap tried a third time to break through these fortifications at Phat Diem south of Hanoi, with similar results. This also caused a further attack, with General de Lattre issuing orders to counter attack, killing an estimated 10,000 Viet Minh. This caused questions to be asked inside the Communist Party.

In 1952, General de Lattre fell ill and returned to France. The French appointed General Salan. The Viet Minh continued to harass and attack French supply lines with raids, skirmishes and other guerrilla tactics.

The French continued to develop defences known as Hedgehogs. The idea is that each point of the defensive area could be protected by another point. If done well, it could also allow the defenders to get in behind the attackers, causing them to be attacked from all sides.

The situation was becoming critical for the French. The Viet Minh were having success in the areas in front of the defensive lines and by October the Viet Minh had control of the Black River Valley and most of the Tonkin region. They left the defensive line and successfully attacked Viet Minh supply depots. Nevertheless, this did not stop or majorly effect the Viet Minh operations.

By 1953, General Giap had changed strategy and invaded the country of Laos, extending the war. The French responded by taking the area of Điện Biên Phủ: a heart-shaped valley, with a local population that supported the French, an airstrip and with the ability to disrupt the Viet Minh supply lines to Laos. There was one thing that the French had not anticipated and General Giap had seen: the hills could be taken and would overlook the airfield.

Ho Chi Minh had sent letters to President Truman asking for independence and support and saying that he felt that both countries had similar aspirations for mutual understanding and for a world of peace. These letters were never given to President Truman.

Ho Chi Minh had also attended the peace conference in Paris, France.

The diplomatic situation was complex. Eastern Europe had come under communist control and China was now communist. The Russians had developed nuclear capabilities.

America wanted to stop further expansion into Asia and Europe and had seen Chinese and North Korean aggression in the invasion of South Korea. The spread of communism needed to be stopped.

'We are fighting in Korea for our own National security and survival.' President Truman.

However, the right for countries to be independent and to choose their own future was part of American history. They too had been a colony and gained their freedom through violence and war.

By 1953, the French and Ho Chi Minh began talks to end the fighting in Vietnam. Before the negotiators met in Geneva, both sides pushed to improve their negotiation position by improving their military position. This is where and why Dein Bein Phu becomes important. The French hoped to lure the Viet Minh into a decisive battle.

The victory at Dein Bein Phu inspired the North Vietnamese and had liberated half the country from French occupation.

General Giap, Dien Bien Phu: Rendezvous with History

"Dien Bien Phu was the bell tolling the death knell for colonialism."

Dien Bien Phu was meant to be a stronghold for the French as well as a trap for the Viet Minh, by drawing them out and destroying them in the open. Instead, it would turn into a death trap for the French.

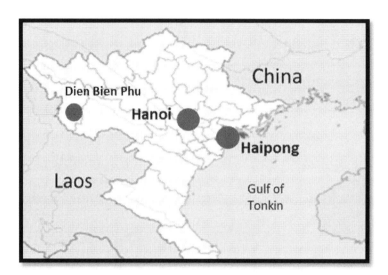

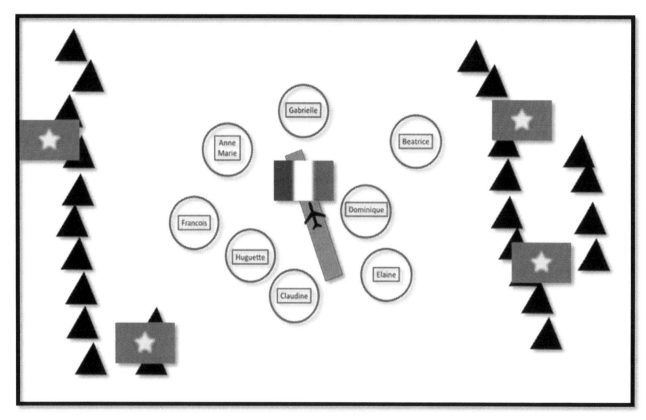

30

General Giap:

'We decided to wipe out at all costs the whole enemy force.'

The French soon lost control of the hills around Dien Bien Phu. What they did not expect is that the Viet Minh would be able to take artillery up to the top of the hills, nor were they expecting the Viet Minh to have anti-aircraft guns. This is considered one of the greatest logistical feats in military history. The Viet Minh surpassed themselves and their opponents' understanding of them. Roughly 250,000 civilian supporters, 50% women, moved everything needed for the battle on foot. Not only did the artillery make it up to the top of the hill, but it was also built into the hills and camouflaged so well that it could not be seen from the air. The Viet Minh dug deep fortifications and they also managed to get anti-aircraft guns. As you can imagine, this makes the defending of Dein Bien Phu very difficult, if not impossible. The area would be bombarded, cut off from the land, and aircraft would be shot down.

France	Viet Minh
20,000 men, (troops)	65,000 men (troops)
10 tanks	250,000 supporting civilians.
400 aircraft, but only 37 pilots.	

In November, General Giap ordered an attack on outposts to the south. The French retreat to Dien Bien Phu but were virtually wiped out by the time they arrived. The French begged Americans for support. According to Eisenhower's diary, he did not think victory in this environment was possible, but he sent military planes, without the US flag or markings, flown by private businesses to drop supplies on Dein Bein Phu.

The Viet Minh then moved their focus onto Dien Bien Phu. In March 1954, the North Vietnamese began firing down on the French in the valley. The French artillery commander, who had underestimated his enemy, committed suicide.

They sent troops to attack **Beatrice** first. Beatrice fell within 1 day.

Gabrielle fell the next day.

Three days later, **Anne-Marie** collapsed due to propaganda and the collapse of Gabrielle and Beatrice. Leaflets were dropped into Anne-Marie letting the local Tai troops know that they were fighting on the wrong side. As a result, most of them defected.

31

The last radio transmission from the French at Dien Bien Phu:

"The enemy has overrun us. We are blowing up everything. Vive la France!"

In the final assaults, the Viet Minh used a combination of tactics. They used large numbers of troops to attack. They attacked several locations simultaneously. They used artillery to destroy fortified positions. They used engineers, also known as sappers, to blow up fortifications and defences. They used trench warfare tactics once men were inside the French defence zone.

The French finally collapsed on the 7th of May and the Viet Minh had captured 11,721 prisoners of war. 8,000 were French. They were marched to a prison camp 500 miles away. Of those French troops, only 3,290 returned to France. This seriously weakened the French position in Vietnam, causing them to lose 1/10 of their military in Indochina. The Vietnamese government today claims that its casualties were 4,020 dead, 9,118 wounded and 792 missing. The French estimated 8,000 dead and 15,000 wounded.

The day before the fall, the French and Vietnamese governments began negotiations at the 1954 Geneva convention - the day before the defeat at Dein Bein Phu.

Crazy fact:

In the first bombardment in March 1954, the Vietnamese were firing 50 shells per minute onto the French in Dein Bein Phu.

French Troops parachuting in to Dien Bien Phu. You can see the hills in the background and the impossible task at hand.

Chapter 2

US policy and intervention, 1954–64
Background:

The second part of the Vietnam war was between the ▬ USA and ⬛ North Vietnam; other countries were also involved. By 1956, the French military had left Vietnam. It was started in secrecy and ended 30 years later in American failure. It witnessed by the entire World and involved 5 Presidents from both political parties.

- ✗ More than 58,000 Americans were dead.
- ✗ An estimated 250,0000 South Vietnamese Soldiers died.
- ✗ 1 million North Vietnamese soldiers and Viet Cong were killed.
- ✗ 2 million civilians across the whole of Vietnam, as well as tens of thousands in Laos and Cambodia, died.

This war was over many different things. For some it was a civil war, for others it was a struggle for independence from foreign invasion. For the Americans involved, watching and protesting this would be one of the most divisive periods in American history. For others, the main point was the ideology. America, fearful of other countries becoming communist, wanted to put a stop to it by using all its military might against the North Vietnamese, who were communist.

The map below shows the loose alliance system created after World War 2. The light blue represents capitalist countries and light red shows communist-run countries with ties to both China and the U.S.S.R. With the extremely light red showing countries with dictatorships. This period was known as the Cold War and would continue until the 1990s. Vietnam became a 'Hot Spot' of the Cold War and created a country for the communists and capitalists to fight each other directly and indirectly.

This was a significant conference between several world powers, over the Korean War and the Indochina War. It met in Geneva, Switzerland at the location of the League of Nations. Despite the victory at Dein Bein Phu, the North Vietnamese could not continue to fight without the support of Russia and China. China did not want to become involved in another war as they had lost over 1 million men in the Korean war. The Soviet Union was hoping to ease tensions with the West. In the end, no one was satisfied.

The conference removed France from its colonial control of Indochina. It split Vietnam in two along a line called the 17th Parallel, and this would be a demilitarised zone. This left North Vietnam, which was communist and led by Ho Chi Minh, and the South, which was a quasi-democratic, dictatorship, puppet government led by former emperor Bảo Đại.

The countries of Laos and Cambodia were also created.

To the left is a picture of Vietnam with the demilitarised zone. (DMZ on the map.)

34

The Accords had also stated that elections were to be held in 1956 to elect a national government for a united Vietnam.

However, the United States and former emperor Bao Dai did not sign the Geneva Accords.

In 1954, Bao Dai selected Ngô Đình Diệm as the Prime Minister of South Vietnam. Until 1955, when a referendum, supported by America, was held to decide if South Vietnam was to become a republic or stay as a monarchy. The monarchy was scrapped. The Republic of South Vietnam was born, and Diem remained as Prime Minister.

300 days for free movement was allowed and an estimated 1 million people moved south. 130,000 moved north and an estimated 5,00-10,000 Northern supporters or Viet Minh remained to be potentially used later.

General Giap stated in his memoir:

"The work of peace drew us forward, but the general elections and other points in the Geneva Agreements were never implemented. Our people prepared once again for a new stage in the long march toward independence and unification. That long march would turn out to be more miserable than the one we had just completed."

Eisenhower and the Domino Theory, the formation of South Vietnam:

The idea of the picture above is that if one domino falls, it pushes down the next domino.

President Eisenhower: *"You have a row of dominoes set up. You knock over the first one, and what will happen to the last one is the certainty that it will go over very quickly."*

Domino Theory was the belief of the American government throughout the Cold War; that the only way to stop communism spreading was through money or military interference. From America's perspective, Eastern Europe and China had collapsed to communism.

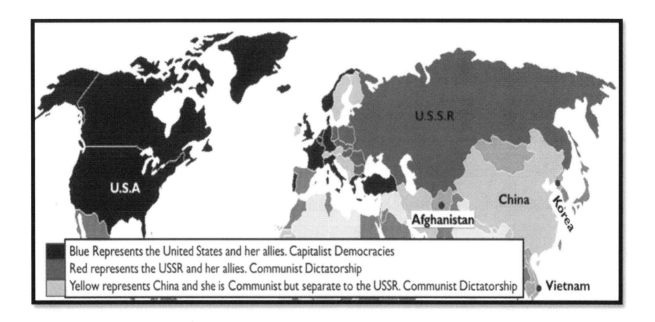

Blue Represents the United States and her allies. Capitalist Democracies
Red represents the USSR and her allies. Communist Dictatorship
Yellow represents China and she is Communist but separate to the USSR. Communist Dictatorship

The only way to stop further communist countries appearing in South Korea and Vietnam was to support the regimes with democracies or dictatorships in charge with military advisors and money. This policy was to be known as **Containment**. However, North Korea invaded South Korea, and the United States and the United Nations sent troops into South Korea and pushed the communist North back to its original borders. This showed the Americans that military actions were effective in retaining democracy and capitalism.

The same seemed to be happening in Vietnam, with the failure of the Geneva Accords and the lack of an election for a national government. North Vietnamese Viet Minh became active in the South and began to attack, using guerrilla tactics and terrorism against South Vietnam.

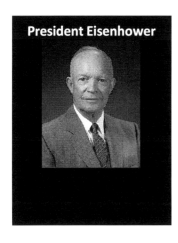

President Eisenhower

"I have never talked or corresponded with a person knowledgeable in Indochinese affairs who did not agree that had elections been held as of the time of the fighting, possibly 80% of the population would have voted for the Communist Ho Chi Minh as their leader rather than Chief of State Bảo Đại. Indeed, the lack of leadership and drive on the part of Bảo Đại was a factor in the feeling prevalent among Vietnamese that they had nothing to fight for."

When reading this quote and looking at the policy of containment and the domino theory, you can see why the Geneva Accords were not signed by either the U.S. or Bao Dai.

Below, US troops 'humping' across a bridge in South Vietnam. 'Humping' means going out from base camp in search of the enemy. They often used the slang term, 'Charlie' to describe looking for the Viet Cong or North Vietnamese troops.

Life in North Vietnam under Ho Chi Minh:

There was a massive change in society in North Vietnam. The government had become communist and this aimed at creating a more equal society. However, this was not going to be easy. For over a decade, the North had been devastated by war.

One of the major concerns had been agriculture. The North is a heavily mountainous region, with little arable land and with a history of most of its food coming from the southern region. This meant that agrarian reforms were vital and came in two forms: "rent reduction" and "land reform."

The land reform redistributed land for 4 million Vietnamese and 8 million benefitted from rent reduction. This was not meant to be a redistribution of land, this was to convert people from independent farmers into co-operatives. The idea is that you work together to decide what to plant and grow and be available to help on each other's farms. By 1961, 85% of farms were now co-operatives. By the 1980s and 1990s, co-operatives were mostly abandoned. It is estimated according to Hungarian and Vietnamese documents, around 13,500 people were executed in order to achieve this agrarian reform.

By 1960 the agricultural reforms were yielding significant results. More than 40,000 co-operatives existed over 90% of the country's farmland. Rice production had doubled to 5.4 million tons. There was growth in other foods, including sweet potatoes, corn and beans.

As many as 500,000 people died during the land reform and communist re-education. Even Ho Chi Minh in 1956, stated that the anti-landlord campaign had gone too far. Anyone could be sent to re-education camps in the North: academics, Catholics, Buddhists, middle and upper class as well as anyone speaking out or questioning the regime.

Accounts from the time vary; living in cities was dangerous once the American's officially joined the war. Bombing raids were significant, causing industry development to struggle. This meant there was a limited amount of electricity; some accounts claim only four hours a day. There was access to radios, newspapers or public loudspeakers, however, they were government-controlled.

Nguyen Dai Co Viet, a professor at Vietnam National University:

"Cameras belonged to the country, so they would give them to only a few journalists to take pictures of battle,"

Tran Van Thuy, a former Viet Minh war journalist:

"My bosses instructed me to shoot anything showing that the enemy would lose,"

With the economy, there was significant improvement by 1960:

- ➢ Over 100 new factories constructed.
- ➢ Coal was being mined.
- ➢ Electricity was being produced.
- ➢ They could produce their own farm machinery, bricks, building supplies, barges and ferries.
- ➢ Significant infrastructure was being built, including the 'Ho Chi Minh trail.'

From 1954–1956, according to the Pentagon Papers, Prime Minister Diem had created miracles in restoring South Vietnam economically and creating a solid political system.

Due to the Free Movement Agreement in the Geneva Accords, significant numbers of Catholics had moved South. This was to provide a solid base of support for Diem, albeit that most of the country was Buddhist.

The smell of corruption:

In April 1955, President Eisenhower decided to end support for Diem's regime. However, Diem attacked the Binh Xuyen gang, which lasted for an entire week. In the end, Diem's forces succeed, and Eisenhower saw no option but to support him. The French, that week, also decided to begin leaving Vietnam.

Due to these successes, in October 1955, a referendum was held to decide if Diem or Bao Dai would be chosen as the leader of South Vietnam. Supporters of Bao Dai were not allowed to campaign. His brother, Nhu, oversaw the elections. 98.2% voted for Diem. However, in Saigon for example, there were only 450,000 registered voters, yet 605,205 had voted for Diem!

Socially

One of his first acts in charge was to "Denounce the communists." This was a plan from 1955 to 1957 to imprison, torture or kill anyone suspected of being a communist without trial. About 12,000 were killed and 40,000 imprisoned. However, in response, the South Vietnamese Communists took matters into their own hands and started to execute South Vietnamese officials.

From April to June 1955, Diem eliminated political opposition in the form of two religious groups, the Cao Đài and Hòa Hảo. There was also an issue with the Binh Xuyen crime-gang, who was sponsored by the French Government. The French did not want Diem to succeed.

In line with ideas of Diem based on Catholicism and Confucianism, brothels and opium dens were closed. In relation to relationships and marriage, divorce and abortion were made illegal, and adultery laws were strengthened. However, he did allow some traditional festivals to continue.

In 1959, under pressure from the United States and people within Vietnam, Diem was forced to hold elections for a parliament or legislative.

However:

> ➤ Independent candidates were not allowed to be published in newspapers.
> ➤ Public meetings could not be held with more than 5 people.

So, campaigning and publicity were nearly impossible. Bearing in mind this is before the days of the internet!

Economically

Economically, his government planned to make Vietnam more prosperous:

> ➤ To improve infrastructures, such as roads and trains.
> ➤ To develop agriculture with the aim of increasing it by 20-25%,
> ➤ To reduce government debt.
> ➤ Center for Technological Development for Investment, Instruction, and Cooperation, whose role was to support industry.
> ➤ He established schools and universities.

However, Diệm admitted the dependence on US assistance:

"Today, the country is not self-sufficient. We can say that foreign assistance is a kind of compensation for the services our people have provided to the free world to protect SEA market, and to fight against manipulations of international communism".

President Eisenhower had ordered American civilians to go to South Vietnam and help in the economic recovery programs. The Americans had a wealth of knowledge on redeveloping an economy based on their experiences in the United States and in helping Europe recover. Eisenhower hoped that this would win the hearts and minds of the Vietnamese people.

Agriculture was going to be key for the Diem government to be successful. However, the communists had beaten them to it and the rich farmers were going to resist this move. Most of the land was held by a small number of rich farmers who rented land to tenant farmers. The aim was to redistribute the land in a program called: 'land to the tiller.' So, land to the person who grew food in the land, also known as a tiller. However, from 1957 to 1963, only 50% of the confiscated land was redistributed. Out of that, approximately 100,000 out of the one million farmers in South Vietnam profited. This was in part because the rich landlords would divide their property up into smaller lots with family members.

Diem also attempted to rehouse people without homes, ex-soldiers and minorities. He built over 200 settlements in regions of Vietnam that were abandoned or unused in Mekong Delta and Central Highland. He did relocate an estimated 250,000 people but the settlements were still lacking and were often run by ruthless and corrupt officials and landlords.

By 1963 tensions between Buddhists and the Diem government had become strained. The government had been run by Catholics in a Buddhist majority country. On the 25th anniversary of the ordination of Diem's older brother as a Catholic priest, and flags were flown in celebration. On the 2527th birthday of the Buddha, when Buddhists flew their flag, police tore them down. In response, Buddhists organised protests in the city of Hue. the regime sent police to stop the protest and shot and killed 8 protesters. The Diem government then blamed the Viet Cong.

Diem had removed Buddhists from several key government positions and replaced them with Catholics. The Buddhist monks protested Diem's intolerance for other religions and the measures. In response, Diem made moves to silence them.

For many Buddhists, they saw Diem and his government as a direct threat to their beliefs. In a show of protest, Buddhist monks started setting themselves on fire in public places. One of the most prolific was a 73-year-old monk called Quang Duc, who set himself on fire, whilst another monk sat repeating in English and Vietnamese.

'A Buddhist monk becomes a martyr.'

Witnesses saw rich and poor alike dropping any gold they had into the donation buckets. Soon other monks became martyrs. Nhu's wife continued to inflame the outrage:

'Burning monks made her clap her hands.'

42

Army officers, students and Catholics rallied to the Buddhist cause. Many Americans watching this unfold saw that the Diem regime was failing both in the countryside and in the urban areas and that his position in power could not last.

The impact of Ho's policies to unite Vietnam, the NLF, and the Ho Chi Minh Trail:

Ho Chi Minh had always planned for a united Vietnam. He set up policies for the unification and this was linked to the Ho Chi Minh trail mentioned earlier. It is key to remember here that this was not necessarily a war for spreading the ideas of communism. This was a war to liberate the South and the unify the motherland. The ideas were to get rid of foreign influence, something that the Vietnamese were very experienced with. The Chinese, French, Japanese and now the Americans. This was less a war of spreading ideology and more a war of getting rid of oppressors. This is not to say that communism was not spread, or brutally enforced.

After the ceasefire between the French and the Viet Minh had been arranged, 5,000 to 10,000 Viet Minh stayed south to begin political and military operations to cause problems and bring down the South Vietnamese government.

In 1956, a southern communist leader, Le Duan, wrote a plan called "The Road to the South." He suggested that the best way to gain unification was to fight the Americans. This plan was initially rejected, and then in 1957 implemented. This was to be the beginning of the National Liberation Front, famously known as the Viet Cong. They began with a wave of terrorist attacks on civilians in October 1957.

43

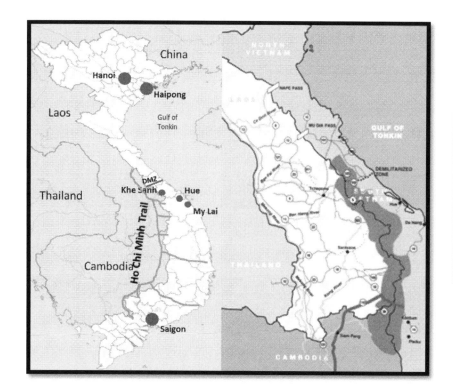

There are two pictures showing the Ho Chi Minh trail.

The one on the left is showing the trail across the country.

The one on the right is showing a close-up and how it was more of a network of roads instead of a single path.

The Ho Chi Minh trail had existed in one form or another for centuries, mainly as primitive footpaths and trade routes. From 1959, it started to become a complex network of supply routes, which contained foot and bike paths as well as roads for trucks. This was started with North Vietnam creating an army group called Group 559. Their motto is below:

"Build roads to advance, fight the enemy to travel."

Group 559's aim was to start infiltrating cadres and weapons into South Vietnam via the Ho Chi Minh trail. The trail would become a strategic target for future military attacks. By 1961, Group 559 and the Ho Chi Minh trail were bringing in thousands of infiltrators/cadres into the South- anywhere between 4000 and 12,500.

By 1964, an estimated 20-30 tons of supplies per day were being brought into South Vietnam using the trail and, by the following year, 234 tons of supplies per day.

The paths were extremely well made but due to the bombing they were heavily camouflaged. It was claimed that by 1973 you could drive the length of the trail and a truck would only be seen by the air when it had to cross streams and rivers. The trail was not just a trail, it contained barracks, hospitals and command centres.

The National Liberation Front is also known as the Viet Cong.

This was a political organisation with an army made up of people based in the South with the aim of converting the non-communists. If was formed in 1960 by the North Vietnamese and was supported by North Vietnam, Russia and China.

Their aims were to:

1. Get rid of foreign control
2. Redistribute land among the peasantry.

According to the American Pentagon Papers, its aim was to:

"Overthrow the camouflaged colonial regime of the American imperialists," and to make "efforts toward the peaceful unification".

It had guerrilla units, regular army units and cadres who organised the people in the countryside.

In the autumn of 1961, the number of guerrilla attacks rose from 50 in September to 150 in October. By 1962, they had 300,000 members.

By 1963, most of South Vietnam's rural areas were under Viet Cong control.

In February 1965, the Viet Cong attacked American air bases and killed American soldiers.

By the end of the war, the Americans had killed an estimated 20,000 Vietnamese working on the Ho Chi Minh trail and had dropped more bombs on it than the number of U.S. bombs dropped during World War Two. Yet they did not stop the traffic on the Ho Chi Minh trail.

One of the slogans/mantras to the Strategic Hamlet Programme:

"Draining the water to catch the fish."

The defences of a strategic hamlet

Diem and his American advisors decided that one of the best ways to deal with the Viet Cong was by building Strategic Hamlets. 80% of South Vietnam's population was based in the countryside, so this was to be a decisive step in defeating the communists.

American news reporter Neil Sheehan, who had visited Vietnam with Robert McNamara:

'I remember going, during one of Robert McNamara's visits, out to one of these hamlets. The Vietnamese General who commanded the area was telling McNamara what a wonderful thing this was. And some of these farmers were digging a ditch around the hamlet. And I looked at their faces and they were really angry. I mean, it was very obvious to me that if these people could, they'd cut our throats.'

The aim was to stop the Viet Cong getting access to the Villagers by separating them with defensive barriers, walls, bamboo spikes, ditches and barbwire, with a security force and a guard tower. The village or hamlet was to be provided funds and support from the government, thus making them unavailable to the Viet Cong and reliant on the government. This was meant to win the hearts and minds of the Vietnamese People. Secretary of Defence, Robert McNamara, had been so convinced of the success that he made the Pentagon draw up plans to withdraw from Vietnam in 1965.

However, the program was rolled out and they attempted to complete in such a short space of time that it was impossible to function. The program started in 1961/1962; according to the Pentagon Papers, 4.3 million had been housed by September and 2000 hamlets were still under construction. However, in December 1963, US officials discovered that only 20% of the hamlets met basic standards. Farmers were forced to abandon their homes to move to the strategic hamlets. Corrupt officials siphoned off funds and the villagers blamed the Diem regime for failing to protect them from guerrilla attacks. As their anger grew, so did the ranks of the Viet Cong. By 1964, the programme officially ended as a complete failure.

Stanley Karnow, an American Historian and Journalist, wrote:

The strategic hamlet built during the previous summer now looked like it had been hit by a hurricane. The barbed wire fence around the enclosure had been ripped apart, the watchtowers were demolished and only a few of its original thousand residents remained, sheltered in lean-tos... A local guard explained to me that a handful of Viet Cong agents had entered the hamlet one night and told the peasants to tear it down and return to their native villages. The peasants complied...

From the start, in Hoa Phu and elsewhere, they had hated the strategic hamlets, many of which they had been forced to construct by corrupt officials who had pocketed a percentage of the money allocated for the projects. Besides, there were virtually no government troops in the sector to keep them from leaving. If the war was a battle for "hearts and minds,"...the United States and its South Vietnamese clients had certainly lost."

The Viet Cong spent time in the countryside, feeding off this anger and their message was, 'Turn your grief into action.' They passed pamphlets and leaflets saying, 'We will fight together, we will get rid of this corrupt and unjust government, get rid of the foreigners, unify the country, and we will bring in this economic and social justice.'

During this period, Ho Chi Minh had been seeking help from China due to the hamlets and the lack of success the North Vietnamese were experiencing in South Vietnam, with concerns that an invasion of North Vietnam was imminent. The Chinese promised to arm and train thousands of North Vietnamese soldiers. The North Vietnamese Politburo also began conscription of all able-bodied men into the army.

August 2, 1964

&

August 4, 1964

Other incidents had happened before this, but the Americans had not retaliated or used it as an excuse to go to war. In 1959, 6 Americans were killed by Viet Cong troops whilst watching a movie in their mess hall. They were arguably the first American deaths of the Vietnam War.

The Gulf of Tonkin was a highly controversial topic, and was two separate incidents, and did not take place. (This is confusing but will be explained later.) On July 30th, 1964, South Vietnamese ships under President Johnson's orders began shelling North Vietnam.

Off the coast of Northern Vietnam, August 2nd, 1964, the destroyer USS Maddox was pursued by three North Vietnamese torpedo boats. The Maddox fired 3 warning shots and the North Vietnamese retaliated.

However, from a combination of United States Secretary of Defence, Robert S. McNamara, and North Vietnam General, Giap, both have stated that the second Gulf of Tonkin attack on the 4th of August never happened. This was only openly admitted in the 1990s and 2000s. Prior to this, President Lyndon Johnson used this as a reason for the United States to enter the Vietnam War.

Yet, privately President Johnson admitted:

"For all I know, our navy was shooting at whales out there."

The first incident had taken place for a combination of reasons. There had been commando raids along the North Vietnamese coast and therefore North Vietnam was looking to stop this. Secondly, according to the French Indochina agreements, the coastal or sea territory that North Vietnam was entitled to be 20 miles or 12 nautical miles. The USS Maddox was in the 12 nautical mile zone and refused to acknowledge the 1936 French-Indochina agreements.

On August 4th, President Johnson announced that the incidents had taken place, that America and South Vietnam were both only acting defensively, and that the events had taken place on the 'high sea,' thus suggesting that the events took place in International Waters.

This was then used to rally Congress to get approval to go to war with North Vietnam, eventually causing the bombing of North Vietnam, Cambodia, Laos and the deaths of 58,000 American Soldiers.

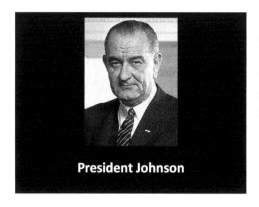
President Johnson

In 1964, President Johnson declared:

"The United States regards as vital to its national interest and to world peace the maintenance of international peace and security in Southeast Asia."

The law gave the President of the United States the right to:

"Take all necessary measures to repel any armed attack against the forces of the United States and to prevent further aggression."

This incident and this law would cause significant problems for the United States socially and politically.

Chapter 3

Confrontation in the Vietnam War, escalation 1964–68

Events:

The Gulf of Tonkin was the final piece for the full escalation of the war and bringing America into the Vietnam Conflict. Yet no declaration of war was made. Yet, Congress did pass the Tonkin Gulf Resolution. The Tonkin Gulf Resolution in 1964 gave the President the powers to send America to war, but it was not a declaration of war. The Americans began a bombing campaign against North Vietnam and the Ho Chi Minh trail.

The Viet Cong was the name of the communist guerrilla army who were partly from the south of Vietnam and from north Vietnam. They mainly used guerrilla tactics to fight because they could not match the strength of the US military, its resources and equipment. The North Vietnamese Army (NVA) and Viet Cong were no match for the USA and the Army of the Republic of Vietnam (ARVN) in open warfare. The leader of the communists was Ho Chi Minh. He had studied the guerrilla tactics used by China's communist leader Mao Zedong in the 1930s and 1940s. Mao had been successful in his struggle against the Capitalist Chinese Nationalist Party. Ho Chi Minh was also experienced in the use of these tactics because he had used them against the Japanese during the Second World War and the French in the years that followed.

These tactics were dependent on the support of the local peasantry who would be expected to hide the Viet Cong. The Viet Cong fighters, in return, were supposed to be respectful to the villagers and, where possible, helpful. However, it is estimated that between 1966 and 1971, the Viet Cong killed 27,000 civilians. They were prepared to kill peasants who opposed them or who co-operated with the capitalists/Americans. They used a variety of tactics including assassinations of police, tax collectors, teachers and other employees of the government of South Vietnam.

US President Johnson:

To begin with, President Johnson continued the previous President's military policy of using military "advisers," nevertheless, Ho Chi Minh sent units of the NVA (the North Vietnamese Army) into South Vietnam to support the Viet Cong. Johnson responded by increasing American involvement. Johnson had inherited a lot from the increased participation of President Kennedy. Kennedy had authorised Agent Orange, Napalm, the increase in funding for the ARVN, helicopters and armoured personnel carriers, and more military advisors. These advisors would not only train the ARVN, but they would also go out on missions with them. This broke the rules created at the Geneva Accords.

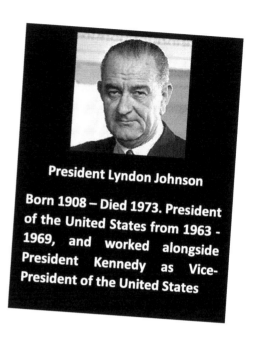

President Lyndon Johnson

Born 1908 – Died 1973. President of the United States from 1963 - 1969, and worked alongside President Kennedy as Vice-President of the United States

After the Gulf of Tonkin incident in 1964, Johnson had and used the excuse to attack North Vietnam, however, this would not be an invasion. Instead, in 1965, he ordered the bombing of North Vietnam. He then ordered US troops into South Vietnam to support the weak ARVN. The President believed that these actions would lead to a quick defeat of the Viet Cong.

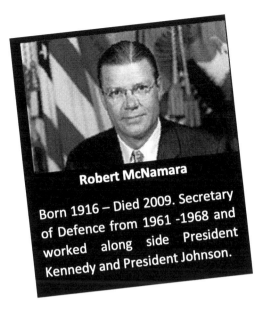

Robert McNamara

Born 1916 – Died 2009. Secretary of Defence from 1961 -1968 and worked along side President Kennedy and President Johnson.

Robert McNamara was made Secretary of Defence by President Kennedy, during the Vietnam War and still under the Kennedy administration. McNamara bought the number of American military advisors from 900 to 16,000. Military advisors were only supposed to train the Vietnamese troops. McNamara also played a key role in pushing forward the Gulf of Tonkin incident as a way of getting the US military involved in the Vietnam conflict.

In 1965, McNamara and other US military officials pushed for further military involvement. His plan eventually led to 485,000 troops being involved by the end of 1967 and almost 535,000 by June 1968. This was possible by allowing conscription in the United States.

Westmoreland:

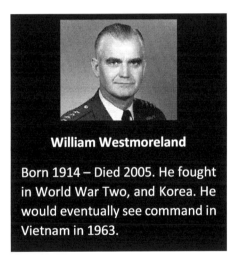

William Westmoreland

Born 1914 – Died 2005. He fought in World War Two, and Korea. He would eventually see command in Vietnam in 1963.

In March 1965, 3,500 marines arrived in Vietnam. From now on, General Westmoreland directed the war in Vietnam. By 1968 there were over 500,000 US troops in South Vietnam.

Westmoreland's plan was to kill so many Viet Cong and NVA that the communists would give up. This is known as a war of attrition. However, this is something that the public and politicians would not want. The second part of his plan was to implement a new anti-guerrilla warfare strategy known as 'Search and destroy.'

Westmoreland and McNamara had similar views about statistics and their importance in winning a war. Westmoreland felt that because US casualties were almost always much smaller than those suffered by the Viet Cong and North Vietnamese Army.

However, the North Vietnamese leaders were willing to accept massive casualties and planned to wear down the US for as long as necessary.

53

This photograph shows a Viet Cong soldier being dragged out of his trench by US soldiers.

If he had not been caught, he may have ambushed or set a booby trap to catch the Americans and anti-communist natives.

Since the Viet Cong had the support of the locals, there was a 'wall of silence' when the Americans asked for help from the local people.

Che Guevara was a political guerrilla fighter in South America and Cuba.

"Why does the guerrilla fighter fight? We must come to the inevitable conclusion that the guerrilla fighter is a social reformer, that he takes up arms responding to the angry protest of the people against their oppressors, and that he fights in order to change the social system that keeps all his unarmed brothers in ignominy and misery."

The Viet Cong were clever and skilful in the way they fought the Americans. They knew they could not match the American resources, so they used Vietnam's jungle environment to their advantage. Philip Caputo, a US marine who fought in Vietnam stated:

"It wasn't so much the Viet Cong that were intimidating at that point as it was the terrain. Going from Point A to point B was so difficult. It took four hours to get half a mile."

The Viet Cong could lay in wait and hide from the Americans. This tactic aims to use small groups to attack the enemy by surprise, then disappear into the surrounding countryside. Eventually, this would wear down the American forces and destroy their morale.

The Viet Cong were almost impossible to identify. Since they had the assistance of most of the local population, they could quickly be assimilated back into village life. They also dressed similarly to Vietnamese civilians and so it was hard for the Americans to identify their Viet Cong enemy.

They built a vast network of underground tunnels, storage bases, workshops, kitchens, hospitals and barracks. They were able to operate and exist without outside support and provided not only refuge from the bombing but also a haven for the guerrilla fighters.

The entrances were developed in such a way that they could easily disappear into the jungle.

Below is a before and after picture of the tunnels. Can you see the entrance?

Imagine walking through the jungle trying to find this; it would be nearly impossible.

Special Units were created to go down these holes and attack the Viet Cong inside. They were called: Tunnel Rats.

The tactics aimed to wear down and destroy an enemy soldier's morale. This was very effective, as soldiers were in continuous fear of ambushes and booby traps.

'My hatred for them was pure. I hated them so much and I was so scared of them. Boy, I was terrified of them and the scared I got, the more I hated them.' John Musgrave, US Marine, served in the Vietnam War at the age of 18.

In fact, 11% of American deaths were caused by booby traps and 80% of all casualties (wounded and deaths) came from booby traps. These were cheap, easy to make and useful. For example, sharpened bamboo stakes, hidden in shallow pits under sticks and leaves. The bamboo was so sharp that it could easily pierce a boot. Cheap, easy to make and hard to find.

Simple, easy to build and cheap, this is a replica of the traps built in Vietnam, we've already seen they were impossible to find, in this picture we can see how deadly they were. Bamboo would be used and could be sharp enough to cut straight through your boots.

The tunnels were booby-trapped, and generally a death trap for US and ARVN forces.

Below is an image of a Viet Cong set of tunnels. We looked at the entrances earlier in the ground. However, you can see below that the entrances could also be underwater or based within a building.

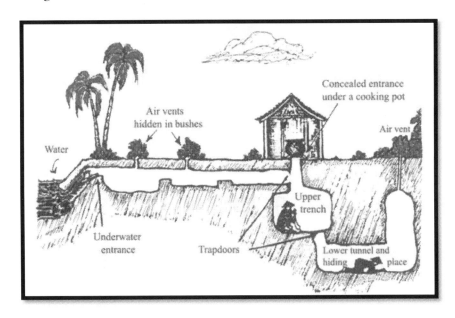

The image has limitations though, as it gives the impression that they are straight tunnels. They spread themselves out in different directions, moving left and right. The tunnels of Củ Chi are 75 km, complex, and were the base of operations for the Tet Offensive. Over 250 kilometres of tunnels were built in Vietnam, some of which passed under US military bases.

Weird fact:

The estimated 250 km of Viet Cong tunnels is roughly the same circumference as the whole outer edge of London. Imagine digging a tunnel that long!

Search and Destroy from 1966 to 1967:

This was the second phase of Westmoreland's strategy to defeat the Viet Cong. American army units were sent to a fortified location. From there, they would go into the villages and the countryside to search for and kill any Viet Cong. They would set ambushes near to the Viet Cong bases or routes they used.

Search and destroy missions were backed up by helicopters, which were used to carry troops, arms and supplies. Helicopters were the best form of transport in the thick rainforests and swamps of Vietnam. Helicopters were also used as gunships, armed with rocket launchers and machine guns.

The US Army High Command measured the success or failure of a search and destroy mission by the "body count," meaning the number of Viet Cong killed.

Typical search and destroy tactics being used. Burning down of suspected Viet Cong supporters. These were also known as Zippo missions. This was because a Zippo is a type of lighter, which American troops would use to set buildings on fire.

The bombing campaign:

Presidents Johnson and Nixon both increased the bombing campaigns during the Vietnam conflict. In 1965, the selective bombing was carried out during Operation Rolling Thunder, but as the war intensified this was replaced by saturation bombing, which is dropping bombs on everything. In total there were 15 bombing campaigns, starting in 1965 and running until 1972.

Three times as much explosive was dropped on Vietnam as was dropped on Germany and Japan during the whole of the Second World War. In total, 7,662,000 tons were dropped throughout the whole of the war.

Laos alone had 2 million tons of bombs dropped on it. America dropped 2.1 million tons of bombs on Europe and Asia over the whole of World War Two. This was mainly aimed at stopping the Ho Chi Minh trail that ran through the country.

Operation "Rolling Thunder" started in February 1965. It was intended to be an increasing bombing campaign of North Vietnam with the aim of improving morale in the South and destroying morale in the North. As the bombing increased, the Americans came to hope that the North Vietnamese would want to stop and meet for peace.

President Johnson wanted to keep this quiet from the public because it expanded the war. It saw the bombing of enemy towns, villages and supply lines. It led to thousands of civilian deaths. It was an important tactic as it would draw the communists out and cut off access to food and weapons.

It had four aims:

1. To destroy North Vietnam's transportation system, industrial base, and air defences
2. To halt men and materials coming into South Vietnam
3. To boost morale
4. To get North Vietnam to cease its support for the southern communists

The bombing was also initiated because it did not cost as many American lives as ground warfare. At first, cities like Hanoi and Haiphong were not bombed because Johnson did not want to anger the USSR and China too much by targeting civilians. However, this policy changed, and the USA began saturation bombing.

Despite the huge amounts of bombing, 864,000 tons and it was estimated that it had caused $500 million in damage, the campaign failed because the bombs often fell into the empty jungle, missing their Viet Cong targets. The Viet Cong guerrillas knew the jungle and made use of elaborate underground bases and tunnels to shelter from US bombs and often re-used unexploded American bombs against US soldiers. This became another case of the military thinking about statistics and looking at the efficiency of dropping the bombs over the effectiveness of the bombs on the enemy.

During the operation, Westmoreland requested more troops and President Johnson knew he would be blamed if more American advisors died. He was quoted as saying:

'I feel like a jackass (donkey) caught in a Texas hailstorm, I can't run, I can't hide, and I can't make it stop.'

In 1965, the first ground troops arrived in Vietnam and the South Vietnamese government was not consulted.

This is General Loan, the South Vietnamese chief of the national police. He shot the suspected Viet Cong official Nguyen Van Lem during the Tet Offensive. The photographer, Eddie Adams, reported that after the shooting Loan said, "They killed many of my people, and yours too," then walked away.

These children were running and screaming for help, followed by soldiers of the South Vietnamese army in June 1972. They had been severely burnt by a napalm attack. The photographer won the 1973 Pulitzer Prize winner for this photo. Later in life the girl in the picture said:

"Napalm is the most terrible pain you can imagine. Water boils at 100 degrees Celsius. Napalm generates temperatures of 800 to 1,200 degrees Celsius (1,500–2,200°F)."

This is a Buddhist monk who went by the name of Thích Quảng Đức. In 1963, he decided to protest the South Vietnamese government because of the persecution of Buddhists by the ARVN. He is having gasoline poured on him, and then was set on fire.

The Vietnam War was known as the "first television war". Since the beginning of 1965 and the change in the number of men in Vietnam, the number of journalists also increased. Prior to 1965, there were less than 24 journalists. By 1968 there were over 600 accredited journalists. There were magazines, newspapers, radio and television reporters from all over the world. For the television, the cameramen and reporters would be allowed access to the battlefield (In total 200 reporters were killed during the Vietnam Conflict), they would then return south, and the film would be sent to Tokyo, Japan for editing, and then flown to the U.S.

Although the war was televised more than previous wars, it is heavily debated as to the extent that support for the war was influenced by the news reports. In the initial stages of the war, the media was enthusiastic about the conflict and had portrayed a good-guys versus bad-guys conflict. However, in August 1965, Americans saw a different side of the war. Morley Safer broadcast from the outskirts of a village called Cam Ne. They were on patrol with U.S. marines. Their orders were to search for guns and rice stored there for the enemy, then to destroy it all. Safer recorded the burning of 150 houses, including an old couple's cottage, with images of people crying, holding babies, and no young people to be seen anywhere. The marines had killed 3 women and 1 baby and captured 4 prisoners. Safer then criticised the American actions, stating that the technology could help win the war, but how does that make up for the years of backbreaking labour the people in the village had to do to achieve this standard of living.

He interviewed one of the soldiers involved in this operation and the soldier said:

"I feel no remorse. I don't imagine anyone else does."

The difficultly of this all was whether the reporting reflected the public mood or if the reporting was creating the public mood.

The only correlation that can be seen is that as the causalities increased, the support for the war decreased.

The Tet Offensive was to be the final nail in the coffin for the U.S. government. Having been televised and showing the events unfolding in Saigon and the U.S. Embassy, this caused Americans to believe that the war was not being won. This was further compounded by the American government during 1966 and 1967 as they had been telling the public that they were winning the war in Vietnam, yet somehow the North Vietnamese had infiltrated most of South Vietnam without anyone noticing.

One of the most prolific news presenters, Walter Cronkite, reported in February 1968 that the war was in a *stalemate*:

"To say that we are mired in stalemate seems the only realistic if unsatisfactory conclusion."

Meaning that it was a war without end. President Lyndon Johnson was reported to have stated:

"If I've lost Cronkite, I've lost Middle America."

On March 10th, the New York Times posted that Westmoreland had put in a further request for 206,000 troops. The question being asked by the public and members of government was:

If the Tet Offensive had been an American victory, why were more troops needed?

President Johnson:

'I don't want any dam Dinbinphoo.'

The siege of Khe Sanh started in January 1968 and finished in July 1968. Khe was near the border of the demilitarised zone and Laos. A small group of American soldiers (6,000 marines) and South Vietnamese (ARVN) soldiers fought against a large Viet Cong army.

The area of Khe Sanh had similar importance to Dein Bein Phu. It was close to the border of Laos, contained an airstrip and could be used to stop the North Vietnamese infiltrating into Laos, as well as being built in the philosophy of the strategic hamlets. The area could be used to protect the local population.

From January 1968, the attacks began to increase and from January 2nd to January 22nd the NVA attacked anything that came into the area, including the entire group of American troops coming in by helicopter.

The NVA used artillery, mortars and rockets to destroy American positions and defences. At the beginning of the month, the attacks destroyed the ammunition dump as well as the facility storing the nerve gas.

The situation was becoming so desperate that Westmoreland was considering the use of chemical weapons or nuclear weapons.

The air force used other technological advances instead, to make their bombing more accurate. 316 listening and movement sensors were dropped. These allowed the aircraft to know where the NVA were moving and therefore created more accurate bombing raids. In the end, 14,223 tons of bombs had been dropped in the Khe Sanh.

The NVA changed tactics and reverted to the same tactics that they used at Dein Bein Phu, and started to build trenches, which would move closer to the American base. Eventually, the pressure and the attacks were too much and the Americans withdrew between June and July. The North Vietnamese claimed victory and the American's claimed it was a tactical withdrawal.

This was one of the bloodiest urban battles of the Vietnam conflict, from January until March 1968. An urban battle is a battle that takes place in a city or town. Hue was an important city for a variety of reasons; it was one of the major supply routes and bases for the ARVN.

The city was split in half by the Perfume river and contained an ancient and large citadel to the north of the river.

The attack started with the Viet Cong surprising and killing the guards at the gate to the city, moving through the sewers and capturing both sides of the city. Only two locations held out against the Viet Cong; one American base south of the river and one ARVN base inside the citadel.

In response, a US army to the south moved to recapture the city. However, this was urban combat and this needs special training. Some troops had not been trained for this. Urban combat is one of the most difficult and dangerous forms of combat and takes a long time. Every house becomes a battlefield. You must go into each house and look everywhere for the enemy, and you don't know the house or what is behind each door. As you can imagine from this description this is stressful, and to do a complete city is a nightmare.

The lack of experience caused problems for the US army from top to bottom, as it was not just the troops that were lacking experience. Therefore, general orders were given to just clear out the city any way you can. With one exception, the city was ancient and considered sacred, so monuments and religious buildings were not to be attacked, and this meant that artillery and air support was limited.

However, if they suspected any house to contain enemy troops, they had permission to destroy the house. In order to move from house to house, you would have to cross the street at some point, and this also proved problematic as you were out in the open. The marines had smoke grenades, which did exactly that. They would release large amounts of smoke so that the enemy could not see you. However, as soon as you threw one smoke grenade, enemy snipers and machine gunners would open fire.

On February 2nd, the marines made it to the provincial headquarters, but it would take another 4 days to capture it. This still left the citadel; however, this contained the Imperial Palace and similar instructions were given for not using artillery and airstrikes. With its thick walls and large buildings, it was going to be even harder than the rest of the city. However, by the end of the day artillery had to be brought in, except for the area around the palace. The Viet Cong had planned the defence so well that it was impossible for the marines to get a foothold in the citadel. The fighting finally came to a stop on February 28th. In total, the ARVN and the US lost 668 troops and 3,707 were wounded. For the Viet Cong, the numbers range from 2000–8000 killed and wounded; only 98 were captured alive. In total, 80% of the city had been destroyed, 6,000 civilians died, 1,900 wounded, 110,000 had lost their homes and 2,000 to 4,856 were executed by the Viet Cong. The belief was that they were killed so they could not identify Viet Cong members.

The Tet Offensive:

A massive defeat for North Vietnam was going to turn into a key reason for the final victory. The Tet Offensive started on 31st January 1968. It had long been established that the 31st of January was a Vietnamese holiday and that there was to be a cease fire on this holiday. It was totally different from the guerrilla fighting they had used before and was a surprise attack. Viet Cong forces, supported by the North Vietnamese Army, would simultaneously attack military bases and cities all over the south.

In 1968, the North Vietnamese used the event to their advantage. A huge area of South Vietnam was attacked, including 34 of South Vietnam's provincial capitals, the 6 largest cities in the country, as well as other cities and towns and dozens of military bases, by 84,000 North Vietnamese troops. Part of the North Vietnamese thinking was that most of the ARVN would be away on holiday with their families.

The La Duan and the communists felt that this would make their targets easier to attack and that it would have a significant effect on the morale of the ARVN, South Vietnam and America. They also expected the people to join them with uprisings against the Southern government and America as well as the collapse of the ARVN.

According to one North Vietnamese General:

 "All our thinking was focused on finishing off the enemy. We were intoxicated by that thought."

The Viet Cong began planning over several months beforehand, and in the coming weeks, Viet Cong members checked into hotels or stayed with other Viet Cong based in the city. Supplies of weapons were brought in via vans containing household goods, flower carts and false-bottomed trucks; then buried in fields, cemeteries and garbage dumps. The attack on Khe Sanh was part of this plan, to draw American and ARVN troops away from the south to act as a diversion.

Interestingly, Westmoreland had predicted this attack and had messaged the U.S. government about the impending attack but felt the cities would be the distraction and Khe Sanh was the distraction.

During the build-up, in the city of Qui Nhon, 11 Viet Cong agents were caught with tapes calling on the local people to revolt against the South Vietnam government. Yet still little to no notice was given.

One of the key buildings that the Viet Cong attacked was the American Embassy in Saigon. Although it was not captured, it was all caught on camera, which was then relayed back to the American public and this did not help the war effort. The Viet Cong did not gain access inside the embassy, but they did hold the grounds outside the embassy for 5 hours.

Over 100,000 people were killed during the battle. In total, 20,000 Viet Cong were killed, and 200 Americans were killed.

The effects of the Tet Offensive:

It was a **failure** because:

1. The Viet Cong lost 47% of their troops; 58,000 men and women were thought to have been caught, killed or wounded.
2. The ARVN lost 5% and the US lost 2%
3. The North Vietnamese saw it as a failure, especially as the South Vietnamese did not join in the rebellion and uprising. As a result, they agreed to peace talks after the Tet Offensive.
4. From now on, the NVA did most of the fighting. The Viet Cong never recovered from Tet.

However, it was a **success** because:

1. Before Tet, Americans had been quite confident about the war. The US media had given the impression that the war would be over soon.

2. After the offensive, many Americans felt deceived by the army because Viet Cong troops were shown inside the US Embassy. It seemed that the war could not be won, or at least not for a long time.

3. Most Americans became convinced that the war had to be ended as soon as possible. General Westmoreland, who saw Tet as a victory over the Viet Cong and NVA, was refused more troops.

4. Tet also played a large part in Johnson's decision to give up hopes of standing as President again. President Johnson's popularity dropped to an all-time low.

This would lead to Richard Nixon being elected, as he had promised to end the war.

General Giap was against the offensive and stated that the Tet offensive had been a:

'costly lesson, paid for in blood and bone.'

Helicopters would become one of the most iconic images from the Vietnam War, as well as one of the most versatile and heavily used piece of equipment for the U.S. and ARVN.

Chapter 4

Nixon and Ford's Policies, Vietnamisation, Peace and Communist Victory 1969–75

'The killing in this tragic war must stop.' President Nixon

A poster from the 1960s presidential elections.

By 1968, there were over half-a-million US troops in Vietnam.

The US army was not able to defeat the communists with their superior knowledge of the land and support from the people. At this point, the American public was opposed to the war and began to protest.

Many American troops were being killed or injured and this contributed to a strong anti-war feeling in the USA.

Richard Nixon, an experienced politician including 8 years as Vice-President under President Eisenhower, managed to become President of the United States in 1968. He had campaigned on the promise of stopping the Vietnam conflict. The new president decided to replace US troops with South Vietnamese soldiers, but this still did not defeat the Viet Cong. In 1973, a peace agreement was signed between the USA and North Vietnam, which ended the war. In 1975, the communists defeated the South and the whole country became communist.

There were several reasons why the Paris Peace talks had been started:

For both sides:

1. No sight of Victory for either side.
2. Casualties of the War. For the U.S. 58,000 dead, 850,000 with severe psychological problems, 30,000 wounded and 75,000 severally disabled.
3. Cost of the war. $167 billion for the U.S. so far.

For North Vietnam.

4. Possible loss of aid from USSR and China.
5. Continued bombing of Vietnam.

For the USA.

6. Reduced funding from Congress.
7. Growing anti-war feeling at home.

The Paris Peace Talks had already been going well. President Johnson had stopped the bombing in Vietnam as a sign of good will and because of the progress being made at the Peace Agreements.

However, on November 2nd, the South Vietnamese Government, under President Thieu, refused to go to the proposed talks.

A representative from the Nixon campaign had contacted President Thieu to stay away from the talks and promised that once Richard Nixon was elected, he would negotiate a better deal than the Democratic candidate Humphrey would.

President Johnson became aware of this because of wire taps and secret listening devices inside President Thieu's government.

President Johnson contacted Nixon's office and threatened them with treason charges. President Johnson held a phone call with the Republican Senator Dirksen who was part of Nixon's presidential campaign. The transcript of the conversation is below:

President Johnson: I don't want to get this in the campaign.

Republican Senator Dirksen: That's right.

President Johnson: And they oughtn't to be doing this. This is treason.

Republican Senator Dirksen: I know

President Johnson: And I think it would shock America if a principal candidate (Nixon.) was playing with a source like this on a matter this important.

Republican Senator Dirksen: Yeh

President Johnson: I know this, that they're contacting a foreign power in the middle of a war.

Republican Senator Dirksen: That's a mistake.

President Johnson: And it's a damn bad mistake.

President Johnson also spoke with Richard Nixon, who lied to President Johnson about having any involvement or knowledge of the sabotaging of peace talks. President Johnson knew he was lying. However, he could not go public with the knowledge because it would also lead to questions on how they obtained the knowledge. Nixon escaped treason charges and won the presidential election. By doing this, he killed 35,000 Americans because he stopped the peace talks with North and South Vietnam.

Once Nixon was elected President of the United States, the peace talks resumed but arguing erupted. For example, North Vietnam wanted a four-sided table for the negotiations. One side for the Viet Cong, North Vietnam government, America and the South Vietnam Government. The South Vietnam government demanded the North Vietnam Government and Viet Cong sit on the same side. The sides could not agree and for 10 weeks there was a standoff. In the end, the Soviet Union came up with the solution of having a round table.

In April, the Nixon administration had introduced a new demand. They wanted all American prisoners in North Vietnam to be released and the North Vietnamese had given a detailed report as the history of the prisoners as well as the information of all prisoners alive or dead captured by the North Vietnamese. Once this was completed, they would begin to negotiate the withdrawal of American troops.

Nixon wanted to use this for political play, allowing him to continue the war and escalate if necessary and providing good reasons for its continuation to the anti-war movement. He suggested that the anti-war movement was more sympathetic to the Viet Cong than the American airmen who had been captured and were being held in terrible conditions. The movement at home was successful in gaining support for Nixon's war effort, with American families of missing soldiers being flown into the Paris Peace Conference to confront the North Vietnam government and 5 million tin/copper bracelets with the names of missing airmen being sold. Over the next 4 years, 50 million missing in action (MIA) or prisoner of war (POW) car stickers were sold.

In the end, the four-way talks would get nowhere and President Nixon authorised Henry Kissinger to hold secret meetings with the North Vietnam government.

Widening the War in Cambodia and Laos: 'Secret Bombing':

Nixon's promises during his election campaign had been one of peace, so he was hesitant to start bombing campaigns in North Vietnam due to not wanting to anger American supporters back home. Instead, he secretly started bombing campaigns in Cambodia against Viet Cong bases, which had been protected by the Cambodian government for years.

Nothing was told to Congress, Nixon's cabinet (at least to begin with) or the American public. In May, the Washington Times released an article claiming that the secret bombings were taking place and the government denied all knowledge of the bombings.

The operation was called 'Operation Menu.'

Nixon, in response, authorised illegal wiretapping of 17 reporters and government officials to find out who leaked the reports.

In April 1970, Nixon announced that 30,000 American and 50,000 ARVN troops had invaded Cambodia. Cambodia had recently been taken over by a coup. The previous president had allowed the Viet Cong to exist in Cambodia, but he had not protested the American Government bombing the camps in Cambodia. The new President of Cambodia, Lon Nul, was anti-communist and was backed by the United States.

At the end of the campaign, the Americans had killed 11,349 enemy troops, captured 22,000 weapons and destroyed 11,688 bunkers and buildings.

Nixon's plans for his administration were to ease tensions with the Soviet Union and to open trade and negotiations with China. Previous U.S. governments had refused to recognise the government of China since 1949 and had instead recognised the island and government of Taiwan as the real government of China. However, the ongoing war in Vietnam threatened those plans. 37,563 Americans had died in Vietnam when Nixon became President.

Nixon was quoted to have said in May 1969:

'I am not going to end up like LBJ, holed up in the White House, afraid to show my face on the street. I'm going to stop that war, fast.'

Once in power, Nixon began to look to build relations with China. In July of 1971, Nixon announced that he would be visiting China. In February of 1972, Nixon arrived in China. This had effects on both the north and south. Both governments relied on support from China for the north and America for the south.

By the end of the war, China had 320,000 of its own troops in North Vietnam, freeing up North Vietnamese troops to go south.

The Roles of Kissinger and Le Duc Tho in the Paris Peace Talks (1972):

Henry Kissinger was President Nixon's national security advisor. He was known for having taught government at Harvard and his foreign policy philosophy was based on pragmatism, not ideology.

Henry Kissinger

In 1969, Henry Kissinger had been authorised to meet with the North Vietnamese government. They met in Paris and the Viet Cong and South Vietnamese were not included in the talks.

North Vietnam, according to Kissinger, was stubborn. Their representatives would not even admit to having troops in South Vietnam, and if they would not admit to that how could North Vietnam agree to withdraw them. Henry Kissinger informed them that if their position did not change by November, President Nixon would

"Consider steps of grave consequence."

Le Duan:

In February 1970, in Paris, Kissinger started new secret negotiations with the North Vietnamese. Le Duc Tho was to represent Le Duan and the North Vietnam government. Le Duc Tho openly disliked Nixon's Vietnamisation programme.

In 1971, Henry Kissinger made significant concessions to the North Vietnamese. They could keep their troops in the South and, in exchange for prisoners of war, all American troops could be withdrawn in 7 months.

Le Duc Tho

Le Duc Tho countered and offered the release of all American prisoners with the Americans leaving Vietnam as well as removing the President of South Vietnam, Thieu.

In October 1972, before the elections, and after the North Vietnamese had failed the 'The Easter Offensive' or 'The Summer of Flames,' Henry Kissinger was back in Paris, determined to negotiate a deal with the North. The Chinese and Soviets were now putting pressure on North Vietnam. Le Duc Tho and North Vietnam were now more willing to negotiate, and quickly. They made a concession that President Thieu did not have to go. A ceasefire was then agreed, with the Americans completely leaving South Vietnam, the return of all Prisoners of War, and the Americans completely stopping the bombing of North Vietnam. President Thieu had not been informed of any of these discussions.

Kissinger returned to the United States and at a White House press conference told reporters that:

"Peace Is At Hand."

The Paris Peace Talks resumed after Nixon won a massive victory to become President of the United States a second time. However, just as the talks had started, Le Duc Tho returned to Hanoi, in North Vietnam. The Viet Cong were enraged that President Thieu could stay and that the 30,000 prisoners were not to be released.

Nixon suspended the talks, continued the bombing of North Vietnam (known as the Christmas bombing) and stated that they were considered offering Saigon air support after the Peace Agreements had been signed.

There was significant world condemnation by figures such as the Pope. The President of Sweden went as far as comparing Nixon and America to Nazi Germany.

In December, North Vietnam agreed to return to the Peace Conference and the agreement was made in 6 days. Nixon, in writing, stated to the President of South Vietnam he had to sign, and America would come to their aid if North Vietnam ever broke the terms of the agreement. They were both awarded the Noble Peace Prize in 1973.

The Renewed North Vietnamese Offensive (1972) 'The Easter Offensive' or 'The Summer of Flames.':

In 1972, in part as a result of Nixon's visit to China, North Vietnam and Le Duan decided to start a new offensive, in a new style. Instead of guerrilla warfare, they would change to conventional warfare bigger than any before. The hope would be to destroy or severely damage the ARVN, to improve the negotiations in Paris as well as the secret negotiations and to show Russia and China they were still worth supporting.

The campaign began in March 1972. Over 120,000 men supported by Chinese and Soviet made tanks and support vehicles attacked at 3 key points: the demilitarised zone, the Central Highlands and west of Saigon. There were only 60,000 US troops left in South Vietnam and very few were combat troops.

The northern section near the DMZ collapsed quickly, with thousands of refugees fleeing south as well as entire units of ARVN surrendering or joining the refugees south.

In response, Nixon began Operation Linebacker. These were massive air attacks on the attacking North Vietnamese.

The North Vietnamese attacking west of Saigon met with ARVN resistance 60 miles from the city at the city of An Loc, which had a road that directly led to Saigon. The North Vietnamese started with a massive artillery bombardment followed by a large infantry and armoured attack. The ARVN were driven to an area no bigger than a mile, and reinforcements and supplies could not get to them. However, the ARVN held out. Air power eventually won the war. The tanks, armour, troops and supplies of the North Vietnamese army were no longer hidden by trees and jungle but were in the open, which was the type of conventional warfare the US Airforce was capable of winning. The North Vietnamese suffered 10,000 casualties and lost most of their tanks and artillery.

Nixon had privately admitted that he knew that the war could not be won and that the war would have to be settled in Paris. He had to find a way to remove American troops from Vietnam, without looking as if America had surrendered. He also believed his long history as an anti-communist could work to his advantage with Hanoi, using this and his ability to use a nuclear bomb. In April 1969, a new term was used: 'Vietnamisation.' The South Vietnam government would gradually take control and responsibility for fighting the North and American troops would start to return home. The Americans brought in 1 million M16 rifles, 40,000 grenade launchers and thousands of vehicles to support the ARVN.

By 1970, and President Nixon's first full year as President, he had withdrawn 115,000 troops from Vietnam. Casualties were down, he had reduced conscription and made it random.

In January of 1973, President Nixon informed the American public that they would be leaving Vietnam. From January 27th, a ceasefire would begin and prisoners of war would be freed across Indochina.

It is important to note that the Paris Peace Agreement was a withdrawal agreement and in effect was not a peace agreement. As you could see earlier, there was still a lot to be resolved. There were North Vietnamese and Viet Cong troops still in the South of Vietnam; this was going to have to be resolved and most likely through combat.

The Effects of Ford's Diplomatic Response:

President Ford

With Nixon's resignation for the Watergate incident, Vice President Gerald Ford became President of the United States. The situation in South Vietnam and its government were hanging by a knife edge. The President had been caught covering up for his men, who had broken into the opposition political parties' headquarters in Watergate and had put wire taps and secret microphones in the building.

They were caught and the president tried to protect these men from the law, lying about his knowledge and of covering up the events. America was focused on this instead of Vietnam, and Congress had removed all funding and military support for South Vietnam, whilst North Vietnam continued to be supported by China and the Soviet Union. On August 9th, Richard Nixon resigned, and Gerald Ford became President of the United States.

Within 3 weeks of the cease fire, there were already 3,000 violations of the Paris Peace Agreement.

President Thieu had ordered the ARVN to take and hold as much land as possible during the cease fire.

The North Vietnamese attacked Tay Ninh near the Cambodian border, hoping to establish a rival capital city in the South. They installed surface-to-air missiles south of the DMZ. They built a new highway within South Vietnam that could take 200 to 300 vehicles and a giant pipeline for fuel.

In December 1974, North Vietnamese forces attacked Phuoc Long, just north of Saigon. They wanted to see what the Americans would do. Within 3 weeks they had overrun the entire area, and the United States did nothing. President Ford had significant problems with the fall out of Watergate. America had problems with inflation, unemployment, tensions in the Middle East, as well as the upcoming impeachment of Richard Nixon. When asked in public if he intended to do anything to support the South Vietnamese, he said that they would only be supplied.

In April, President Ford appealed to Congress for $722 million in emergency and military aid. He even stated that if they refused and Saigon collapsed, Congress would take the blame not the President. Congress refused as they felt that it was too late to make any difference.

In March, the North Vietnamese gained control of the Central Highlands. General Giap was reinstated as overall commander of the North Vietnamese Army. At this point, most ARVN troops were only given 85 bullets per week and 1 grenade. They had no air support and limited fuel for their vehicles. The task they were facing was impossible. The ARVN retreated from the Central Highlands and attempted to regroup and concentrate their forces east of the Highlands, but the North Vietnamese were too much, and the ARVN began to withdraw south, bringing with them 400,000 refugees. This would become known as 'The Convoy of Tears' as thousands would die on this path to Saigon. South Vietnamese pilots accidentally bombed the refugees. The North Vietnamese blocked major roads, forcing the refugee convoy to take back roads, slowing the convoy. They also shelled and attacked the route. This caused refugees to get trampled on by other panicking refugees; there were even accounts of retreating tanks running over the convoy. By March 29th, the cities of Hue and Danang had been captured. The North Vietnamese had made more progress in a day than in 20 years. The North Vietnamese had 18 divisions and 5 in reserve against the South's 6 divisions.

The Americans began to discuss and plan evacuation. There were 5,000 Americans in Saigon and 200,000 South Vietnamese families who had worked with the Americans. There were two options: air, with commercial and military aircraft; and sea, with cargo ships.

In April, 40 miles East of Saigon, Xuan Loc was attacked by North Vietnamese forces and the last city before Saigon. The ARVN commander refused to retreat.

Reporter: You're certain you can hold Xuan Loc?

ARVN commander: 'Surely, Surely, I am certain to you. I am sure with you. I can hold Xuan Loc. Even the enemies use, you, the double forces or maybe three times more than my forces. But no problem sir, no problem.'

On April 21st, Xuan Loc fell to the North Vietnamese and President Thieu resigned. Four days later, he was taken to Taiwan and was not allowed entry into the United States.

On April 27th, Saigon began to be bombed and the main assault began. All American cargo ships were ordered to immediately sail out of the Saigon harbour.

On April 28th, a new South Vietnamese President was sworn in. He had been involved in the coup that got rid of President Diem.

On April 29th, the airport in Saigon, Tan Sun Nhut, was attacked with rockets and artillery. The 2 last American servicemen to die in Vietnam were killed in the attack. The runway was in ruins and had caused the Americans to almost run out of evacuation options. However, there were two spots inside the American Embassy that could support the landing of helicopters. One on top of the embassy building and the other was the embassy carpark. There were other designated spots for helicopter collections points across the city.

More than 50 American helicopters came into the city, taking people from Saigon to the United States Fleet stationed off the Vietnam coast.

On April 30th, the American Ambassador, Martin, left and only Americans would now be evacuated. 400 South Vietnamese remained inside the courtyard. The last American troops and government officials left the embassy at 7:53am. Within 5 hours, the South Vietnamese government and South Vietnam no longer existed, and the President of South Vietnam ordered all troops to stop fighting. Saigon was renamed: Ho Chi Minh City.

Weird fact:

The American Ambassador to South Vietnam refused to believe that Saigon would fall and that the Americans would have to be evacuated even when shelling of Saigon began on April 27th!

This photo was taken on April 29th, 1975. It shows CIA agents helping South Vietnamese evacuees onto an America helicopter just before the fall of Saigon.

Reasons for the Communist Victory:

This should not be in the exam, but it is something that students are always curious about. Guerrilla tactics proved decisive due to several factors:

- ➤ Peasants in Vietnam had been alienated by different American policies, including Strategic Hamlets and Search and Destroy tactics. Many Viet Cong were recruited from the local villages.

- ➤ The American military officers from the very start were having difficulties in understanding what lay ahead as a military conflict. They felt the war was going to be like North Korea, a conventional war, and it was anything but a conventional war.

- ➤ The Americans knew little about the country. The military at the Pentagon, saw the country more of a chess piece in a strategic war against Russia, than a country with a history and culture.

- ➤ The Americans failed to appreciate the enemy's resolve and misread how the South Vietnamese felt about their government.

- ➤ Large numbers of Vietnamese saw no difference in the Americans to the French: that they were in Vietnam to make it a colony.

- ➤ Ho Chi Minh Trail was essential. Supplies from the North were coming to South Vietnam via a set of roads called the Ho Chi Minh Trail that ran through neighbouring Cambodia. There were up to 40,000 Vietnamese working to keep the trail open, and many of the supplies were provided by the Soviet Union and China.

- ➤ Knowledge and understanding of the jungles of South Vietnam. The US attempted to destroy the jungles using chemicals such as Agent Orange. However, this only alienated the local population.

- ➤ Inexperience. The USA had no experience or knowledge of guerrilla/jungle warfare carried out by the Viet Cong. This inexperience was worsened by the fact that most of the US troops, especially after 1967, were not full combat troops but men (nineteen was the average age) who were conscripted into the armed forces and generally served only one year in Vietnam.

- ➤ With the death of Diem, a series of military coups happened, which destabilised South Vietnam, 8 different governments in total.

Chapter 5

The Impact on Civilians in Vietnam and Attitudes in the USA

The Effects of the War on Civilians in Vietnam.

'People sing about Victory, about Liberation. They're wrong. In war, who won and who lost is not a question. In war, no one wins or loses. There is only destruction. Only those who have never fought like to argue about who won and who lost.' Bao Ninh, North Vietnamese Army.

Vietnamese civilians seemed to be caught between a rock and a hard place almost everywhere they went.

North

If you were based in the North of Vietnam, life would be difficult. In the North, you had a brutal communist dictatorship, which would brutally kill thousands of citizens, rich farmers, collaborators with the French, or those questioning or speaking out against the regime. If that was not enough, living standards were low, even in the city where there was limited electricity, as well as the bombing campaigns in the later half of the war. Finally, all able-bodied men were conscripted into the army from 1963. As the war continued and especially after the Tet Offensive, it was clear that the government propaganda did not make sense. If the Tet Offensive had been successful, why were they still fighting? Where were their sons, grandsons, daughters, and granddaughters? Why were American bombers still bombing? Yet if you spoke out, you would disappear. Very few would receive notifications about their relatives' deaths, and the newspapers and radio reports would only discuss the victories.

South

In the South, life would be equally difficult. You were in a family dictatorship. Diem and his brother Ngo Dinh Nhu oversaw the government. Nhu had been the architect of the Strategic Hamlet programme. Although the economic reform had been good, to begin with, the level of corruption had filtered all the way down to the army. The corruption in Diem's regime had filtered down to the commanders in the field as well as local officials, who were taking money for the Strategic Hamlet construction programmes.

Nhu used brutal tactics to control the country and his party. Special internal security units' groups were sent out to spy and kill enemies of the regime. If you spoke out against the regime you would disappear. American reporters who investigated too deeply into the regime could be ordered to leave the country. Nhu's wife was quoted to have said about American reporters being ordered out of the country:

"Vietnam had no use for your crazy freedoms."

The military campaign was causing its own problems, stirring hatred in the countryside. ARVN and Americans used poor tactics in the countryside against the guerrillas, both in taking out the Viet Cong and then causing civilian casualties, which stirred up hatred. Largely because of the inability to tell civilian from Viet Cong. If you killed one Viet Cong member you had one less Viet Cong to deal with. If you accidently killed one civilian, you could create ten Viet Cong. As a result of their inability to tell friend from foe, people in the countryside were brutally and merciless beaten or killed if it was though that they were conspiring with the communists. If a civilian ran away from South Vietnamese troops or Americans, you were with the enemy and could be shot and killed as a suspected Viet Cong member. The amount of hatred and fear that this must have caused to the civilians is unimaginable, not to mention the stress and irritation of the Strategic Hamlets, which meant civilians could be relocated from their family home and then forced to spend time to build structures they felt they did not need. It is clear to see that life for most people in Vietnam during this period was difficult and often brutal. However, unlike the North, after Diem's government collapsed there were still more freedoms than in the North. You could protest and demonstrate, in public and in newspapers, for more freedoms of speech and religion.

There was also a problem with the South Vietnamese economy, which was based around American money being spent by American Soldiers, and towards the end of the 1960s, the money had been so important that the economy itself was based on the need of American money. With this came large amounts of corruption. One report suggested that 10% of goods coming in from the United States were stolen and then sold on the black market. In one year alone, the black market and stealing of goods cost the U.S. Military $2 billion. Officials, ARVN and police could be bought and were not to be trusted. The corruption was everywhere.

When the Vietnam conflict started 80% of the population lived in the countryside. By the end of the 1960s, 50% lived in urban areas. Saigon's population tripled to 3 million. Half the refugees from the countryside had no permanent shelter. Cholera and typhoid killed thousands. Thousands of orphans were in the streets, begging, scavenging, looking for work or pockets to pick. Tens of thousands of women who arrived in the urban areas became prostitutes and bar girls.

US Response to Guerrilla Warfare:

Hearts and Minds:

The Americans needed to win the hearts and minds of the Vietnamese in order to win the war. So, they and the South Vietnamese set up a strategy and several programs to win the hearts and minds of the South Vietnamese population. The French had tried something similar with their 'Pacification programme.' This had failed.

The U.S. strategy was to hold and protect the population and important areas. This was where the idea of the Strategic Hamlet came in.

The strategy for 'hearts and minds' had been started by the British in Malaysia in 1952, and the British had been successful in getting rid of the insurgents.

Under Diem, the programme started with Agrovilles and putting peasants into fortified hamlets.

In 1961, with the Agrovilles failing due to the Viet Cong entering the Agrovilles and killing people, the Strategic Hamlets were started with the aim of the ARVN being stationed nearby to help the hamlets if they were under attack. In the end, the Strategic Hamlets were a big failure.

There was also the Chieu Hoi program ("Open Arms"), which encouraged the Viet Cong to change sides and join the South Vietnamese. This was far more effective. The program involved dropping sealed leaflets into the jungle. The leaflet acted as a pass to any Viet Cong wanting to defect to the South Vietnamese. It is estimated that between 50,000 and 100,000 Viet Cong defected to the South Vietnamese regime. Some of these men were then attached to army units and proved themselves to be invaluable to the war effort, with some of these men winning significant medals and awards from South Vietnam and American armies.

In 1968, the CIA started Operation Phoenix. The aim was to arrest, interrogate, convert and kill suspected Viet Cong activists as well as co-ordinating their information with the South Vietnamese and Australians.

After the Tet Offensive and the other two offensives that happened afterwards, the American's believed that the Viet Cong were now severely weakened. This meant that the ARVN were free to move back into the countryside and attempt to win the support of the local population. The only way to guarantee permanent security was to destroy the Viet Cong political structure. To do that they needed to round up tax collectors, village chiefs, spies and supporters who would then be killed or captured and be persuaded to defect. The only way the Viet Cong coming from the North could work is with this support network.

The targeting would only be as good as the intelligence. The Americans would only act as advisors and building infrastructure such as the 44 provisional interrogation centres built by the CIA. The rest of the operation would be built by the South Vietnamese military.

According to those that were captured and taken to the provisional interrogation centres, they used electric shock treatment, starting with the ear, lip and then tongue and working down the body. They used pincers to pull nails out, brutal beatings and would pour soapy water down the throat.

One of the more notorious prisons was called Devils' Island. Prisoners were kept in rooms 9ft by 5ft, which would contain 3 prisoners.

Between 1968 and 1972, Operation Phoenix captured 81,740 people suspected of being members of the Viet Cong. 26,369 of the 81,740 were killed. However, the programme mainly held low ranking Viet Cong and there was no accountability for the actions. It was even admitted to Congress that the programme did not know if the 26,369 that were killed were innocent. The programme did succeed in degrading the Viet Cong infrastructure; the South Vietnamese government remained unpopular. A poll held in Long A province showed that 35% backed the South Vietnam government, 25% for the NLF and 45% for anyone who opposed the Viet Cong and South Vietnam government.

Part of a letter Ron Ridenhour sent to various people in government regarding the My Lai Massacre:

"I think it was Winston Churchill who said. 'A country without a conscience is a country without a soul, and a country without a soul is a country that cannot survive.'"

On the 16th of March 1968, three US platoons (105 men) landed by helicopter near the village of My Lai. The area was known as 'Pinkville' and was renowned for being a troublesome area, full of booby traps and Viet Cong. The US troops were sent to this area on a search and destroy mission. Over two to four hours, it is estimated that the Americans killed 300 men, women and children. If they ran, they were shot, and it was reported that Lieutenant Calley got the villagers into three groups and killed each group. This killing would have been worse if it were not for a helicopter pilot, Hugh Thompson, who landed in between the American soldiers and the Vietnamese villagers. He ordered his crew to shoot the Americans if they did not stop shooting the civilians.

A mile away, at the same time, another company murdered 97 villagers.

The truth about the massacre did not come out for eighteen months. A soldier by the name of Ron Ridenhour had heard rumours of the atrocities, asked men who had been at Mai Lai separately about the events and they all had the same story. He then wrote to President Nixon, the Pentagon, the state department (they deal with foreign affairs on behalf of the president), The joint Chiefs of Staff, and several congressmen. No one responded. In 1969, Ridenhour was interviewed and told the story of Mai Lai. 14 officers were charged. Only Lieutenant Calley was convicted of war crimes; he only served three years of his life sentence.

Pictures of the massacre were shown around the word and people were appalled. It was another reason why many Americans began to turn against the war.

Three airplanes dropping defoliant in Vietnam

Bombing in Vietnam had been part of both the French and American Army policies. The North Vietnamese also had an air force.

The American bombing campaign came into full force from 1966, with Operation Rolling Thunder.

Napalm

The napalm did clear much of the undergrowth, but it also stuck to humans and caused horrific injuries. It is a petrol-based liquid, which is very sticky, and therefore good for clearing buildings and getting rid of infantry. It was not just militarily effective- it also caused a huge psychological effect. The temperatures and the effect of seeing the huge fire ball of hell would easily terrify most people. It became an infamous bomb that was used over this period. It is estimated that 388,000 tons of napalm bombs were dropped in Vietnam between 1963 and 1973.

Some images from the Vietnam war have become iconic. They also had an effect during the war. In 1966, the anti-war movement protested napalm use, calling for a boycott of the Dow Chemical Company who produced it.

Defoliation:

To help locate the communists in the jungle, chemical defoliants were used to strip trees and bushes of their leaves. The most famous was Agent Orange. Napalm was also used for this purpose.

Agent Orange

From 1962, Agent Orange (2,4,5-T) was used. It gained this name due to the orange strip on its containers. It was a superior strength weed-killer and was used to clear the jungle around military bases and to clear the jungle covering the Ho Chi Minh trail, the route that the Viet Cong used to get supplies from North Vietnam. The Americans had sprayed 20 million gallons of herbicides over ¼ of South Vietnam. It allowed the Americans to see the enemy more efficiently, but it also had the effect of destroying many innocent farmers' crops and killing their animals. The damage is done to soldiers and civilians still rages and still effects people in Vietnam to this day, as well as the ecological impact.

The Effects of the War in the US:

University Protests:

Most campus protests in the 1960s followed a similar pattern:

- Began with a small, often radical, group of students

- Lasted several days

- Often targeted several issues, for maximum support

- Used many of the disruption tactics learned from civil rights protesters (although they also used their own tactics, such as burning the draft cards for the war or going on strike).

- Often, after some negotiation, the campus authorities called the police and there were arrests.

86

Universities across America started to gather momentum in getting out of Vietnam. Students had begun to feel that the universities and the government were stopping the US constitution. Vietnam was not about protecting democracy and The Draft was forcing young American men to join the army.

The Draft was a compulsory order by the government for all men to join the military when they were sent a letter by the government. This could be seen as undemocratic because there was no choice in whether you were to go to war for your country. There were several ways of being able to get out of military service. If you had the money you could avoid the draft, or you could apply to university.

Students in America would have to get a loan or have rich parents willing to pay tuition fees. The costs can be gigantic depending on the university. Thus, one of the big arguments against the war was that the rich could get out of going to Vietnam by paying to go to university.

You could also get out of the war if you could find a medical reason.

There were further problems with few Americans understanding why they were fighting the war. It was difficult for students to understand why troops were flying several thousand miles to go fight a civil war.

During the 1960s, the number of students attending college grew. Towards the end of the 1960s students were protesting in colleges. They were calling for the right to express their opinions and demanding that strict rules be removed. For example, the right to protest and freedom of speech. These are guaranteed by the United States Constitution (a set of laws created at the beginning and creation of the United States). Yet the colleges were refusing to allow peaceful protests to take place on campus, nor were they allowing students to speak out in public on campus about the war.

At first, students protested peacefully, using non-violent methods. However, when this had little effect, many talked of violent revolution.

Student protest had an impact because many of the students involved were middle-class, educated and white.

Students for a Democratic Society

One of the most important activist groups was Students for a Democratic Society (SDS), set up in 1960.

The society drew attention to the values the students had been brought up to approve of (the Declaration of Independence's 'all men are created equal'). However, the reality of life in the USA was very different for minorities and women and both groups were demanding equal rights.

The Students for a Democratic Society campaigned against:

'racial injustice, war and the violation of human rights.'

It was to become the largest student anti-war group, fighting to stop fellow Americans dying for a cause that in their eyes did not make sense. At its height, 6000 people were dying every week from a conflict considered to be illegal, immoral and something that people around the world did not want. In 1962, the SDS released a document known as the Port Huron statement. After its release, support for the SDS grew. Soon campuses were holding demonstrations, with one of the largest being held at the University of Illinois.

As the 1960s progressed, student protests became more organised, more large-scale and more violent. They first achieved national prominence when, in in 1964 and 1965, they organised the 'free speech movement' at the University of California, Berkeley. Nearly half of Berkeley's 27,500 students took part.

The SDS and other student groups began by using the **direct non-violent protest** methods used by civil rights groups. They demanded a greater say in the running of their universities, organised draft-card burnings and occupied university buildings as well as harassing CIA recruiters.

They organised **sit-ins** and other protests over issues ranging from student involvement in university decision-making to the war in Vietnam.

They also organised a **teach-in**, named so because it started with teachers organising the protests. It was a demonstration, led by teachers, which is not limited by time and revolved around current topics, with the aim of eventually concluding an action to be taken. The practice of protesting US policy in Vietnam by holding 'teach-ins' at colleges and universities became widespread. The first 'teach-ins' were seminars, rallies, and speeches. One of the first took place at the University of Michigan at Ann Arbor in March. In May, the 'teach-ins' were broadcast nationally reaching over 100 University campuses.

By the end of 1967, the SDS had about 30,000 members. In April 1968, campuses across the United States held a one-day strike on the 26th. Over 1 million students did not attend class that day. The ability to get this many students to co-ordinate created a large amount of media attention and helped to make the SDS a household name.

The weathermen.

In 1969, a radical group broke off from the SDS and took more direct action; they were known as the weathermen. Their name came from a Bob Dylan song. They staged a 4-day protest in Chicago called "Days of Rage." There was a total of 600 people at the rally. Their aim was for ending the war and instead of starting a revolution. Some of their slogans included:

"Kill all of the rich people."

"Break up their cars and apartments."

"Bring the revolution home."

"Kill your parents."

The Kent State University Massacre:

On May 1st, 1970, students at Kent State University in Ohio protested the escalation of the war in Vietnam with the Invasion of Cambodia. The Vietnam War had been de-escalating, however in April 1970, President Nixon authorised U.S. troops to go into Cambodia, a country next to Vietnam. The students' burnt copies of the Constitution and some draft-cards. Over the weekend there were demonstrations and some violence. The National Guard were called in to keep the peace. On May 2nd, 1,000 students staged a sit in on the campus and a building was burnt down. The Governor of Ohio sent out leaflets informing students that protests were banned.

Student protest became locked in an escalating spiral of violence because:

- The marches and passive resistance actions needed police intervention

- The police became less patient

- The students became more violent and there were more people involved

- Some students saw provoking violence as a way to radicalise more students and gain support.

When there was significant fighting between police and protesters, the state governor usually called in the National Guard. The National Guard were trained as soldiers, not trained for dealing with protesters. On May 3rd, over 1200 National Guardsmen were stationed inside the campus. On May 4th, over 4000 students were now in and around the protest, some protesting, some watching and some going to class. The Guardsmen dispersed

90

the crowds, 28 Guardsmen opened fire at the students and in the air, killing 4 and wounding 9, aged between 19-20.

This tragedy further divided the United States and caused lasting effects on politics. It symbolized what this war was doing to the country, even going so far as killing fellow Americans for expressing their constitutional right to protest and free speech. It almost split the country in half, with groups supporting and others protesting the war. However, according to one Gallup poll, 58% of the people questioned thought that what the guardsmen had done was justified. On the other hand, 4 million students protested the war, and what had happened at Kent State University, 448 campuses closed, and the National Guard was called out in 16 states.

Although the SDS and student protestors did not stop the war, they did help to shift government policy and made withdrawal from Vietnam more likely. Their opposition also did much to influence Johnson's decision not to seek re-election for the presidency in 1968.

Opposition to War in the U.S.A:

There were many issues with the Vietnam War and people in the 1960's began to protest against it.

1. The government had not set clear objectives.
2. It was unconstitutional.
3. Not in the national interest.
4. There had been no declaration of war.
5. The daily body counts shown by the media and the broadcasts from the conflict discouraged many Americans from believing that the war was winnable.
6. One of the biggest parts of the opposition to the war centered around the lack of democracy in the United States, yet the population was constantly being told that they were fighting for democracy and against communism in Vietnam.
7. Troops landing in 1966 and the bombing of North Vietnam.

The roots of the protest can be linked to the college campus protests and teach-ins and they existed before 1965. It was not until the escalation of the war in 1965 that the protests grew in since and significance.

One of the largest protests took place in October 1967, at the Lincoln War Memorial, Washington D.C. and involved over 100,000 people.

The protests gained further ground in December 1969, when the government instituted the first draft (conscription) lottery. This was the first time that this had taken place since World War Two, yet no declaration of war had been made. However, it should be noted that 87% of the marines were volunteers.

Here are some slogans from the time, see if you can figure out what they refer to:

"Dow shall not kill"

"Making money burning babies!"

"Stop the war, feed the poor"

"Girls say yes to men who say no"

"End the nuclear race, not the human race"

"Not my son, not your son, not their sons"

The answers are later in the book.

The different anti-war groups:

We have already mentioned the students, there was also the hippie/hippy movement, African Americans, women, and veterans of the war.

Hippies

"Make love, not war"

Hippies were very anti-establishment, questioned/rejected the values of the previous generation, criticized middle-class values, opposed nuclear weapons and the Vietnam War. They wore ethnic clothing, grew their hair long, grew beards, used drugs, followed mystical religions and explored 'free love'. The ideas of peace and love were symbolized with the idea of Flower Power. They lived in communes, and San Francisco became the hippy capital. They were active in opposing the Vietnam War. They led teach-ins, organizing political action groups, and refused to serve in the military as well as organizing draft-card burnings.

One of the biggest events to take place centered around the hippie movement was the Woodstock Festival that held over 500,000 people on a small dairy farm.

African Americans

Mohammed Ali, one of the most famous athletes in the world at the time, stated about the Vietnam War:

"Why should they ask me to put on a uniform and go ten thousand miles from home and drop bombs and bullets on brown people in Vietnam while so-called Negro people in Louisville are treated like dogs and denied simple human rights?"

Ali risked his career and prison for resisting the draft in 1966.

The war was opposed by Malcom X, Martin Luther King Jr, Stokely Carmichael and the Southern Christian Leadership Conference (SCLC). Dr King was the main leader of the African-American civil rights movement as was opposed to the Vietnam War.

"If America's soul becomes totally poisoned, part of the autopsy must read "Vietnam."

It was felt that America's black community were disproportionately being enlisted into the Vietnam Conflict and young black men were twice as likely to be killed. A complaint was lodged from civil rights groups with the department of defence, and they succeeded in balancing the death count. However, there were still reports of African-American soldiers being treated differently. Wealthier white men could avoid the draft by going to university or to Canada.

Social Welfare Programmes failure

The war took money away from social welfare programmes for the poor, which predominantly effected black Americans.

Women

The position of women in the early 1960s: women still had a second-class status within many protest organisations and businesses. There were large numbers of female protest groups created against the Vietnam War, such as Another Mother for Peace, National Organization for Women, Women's Liberation, Women for Peace, Women's International League for Peace and Freedom (WILPF), and Women Strike for Peace (WSP).

Women for Peace showed up at the White House every Sunday for 8 years from 11am to 1pm for a peace vigil.

In 1968, NOW led by Betty Freidan supported the "Writers and Editors War Tax Protest" pledge. This was a refusal to pay tax in protest of the Vietnam War.

Another Mother for Peace actively worked against nuclear and chemical weapons use during the Vietnam War, and their logo and pamphlet was so popular that they sent between 130,000 and 400,000 pamphlets to homes every year.

Veterans Stage Anti-War Rally

Veterans from World Wars I and II, along with veterans from the Korean War, stage a protest rally in New York City. Discharge and separation papers are burned in protest of US involvement in Vietnam. Three weeks after Lieutenant Calley of the My Lai Massacre was found guilty, 2000 members of Vietnam Veterans Against the War and their followers protested in Washington D.C. This group escalated when 700 veterans again came to Washington D.C. and visited Congress with the aim of returning their medals. They found a large fence had been erected to stop them from gaining entry. In response, the Veterans came up on stage, one by one, and threw their medals over the fence and onto the steps of Congress.

Upheaval at Democratic Convention in Chicago 1968

The frazzled Democratic party prepared to hold its nominating convention in Chicago. Protesters and city officials prepared for demonstrations. In total, 15,000 demonstrators were in Chicago. Mayor Richard Daley ordered in 12,000 Policemen, 6,000 Army troops, 6,000 National Guardsmen and 1,000 members of the CIA and FBI. He denied protester applications for demonstrations near the convention or parks. As the nation watched on television, the area around the convention erupted into violence. On the second night, police drove protesters out of Lincoln Park with clubs and tear gas. The leading candidate was Hubert Humphrey, and he had been the Vice President. The controversy came when during the convention a vote was held on whether there should be support for the Vietnam War. Humphrey's supporters voted no, and the convention erupted into a demonstration. Over the following days the Democrats, Chicago and the United States appeared to the be split down the middle of what to do about the Vietnam War.

Here are some slogans from the time, see if you can figure out what they refer to:

"Dow shall not kill"

This is the name of a company called The Dow Chemical Company that made Napalm.

"Making money burning babies!"

Referring to the called The Dow Chemical Company and Napalm.

"Stop the war, feed the poor"

Refers to President Johnson's plan to implement a social welfare programme for the poorest Americans but because of the Vietnam War, there was no money for this social welfare programme.

"Girls say yes to men who say no"

Men were drafted into the army by conscription. The suggestion is that women would prefer you if you did not join the Vietnam War.

"End the nuclear race, not the human race"

This relates to the nuclear arms race between America/Democracy and Russia/Communism. The planet at this point had enough nuclear weapons to destroy the entire planet.

"Not my son, not your son, not their sons"

Referring to men having to go fight the Vietnam War.

There was a growing conservative movement in the 1960s and 1970s that believed the Vietnam War was just and necessary. Even in the 1940s, there had been anti-communist rallies, and this had continued throughout the Vietnam War. They pushed for President Kennedy to go into direct action. They pushed and supported President Johnson to increase bombing. They supported Nixon with his policies for withdrawal and 'Peace with honour.'.

There were many instances of Pro-War demonstrators coming to the Teach-ins to give an alternative point of view and show their views of anti-communism. Young Americans for Freedom were and are a conservative youth group founded in 1960 and were opposed to what they perceived to be the radical left. (*They were founded at the home of a gentleman called William Buckley who had a fascinating televised debate with Noam Chomsky, which can be found on YouTube. Chomsky was extremely anti-Vietnam. Worth a watch.*) Y.A.F. supported victory for the United States in Vietnam, were supportive of veterans and clashed with the S.D.S. (Students for a Democratic Society)

There was also 'The National Student Committee for Victory in Vietnam' again small in number they also organised student protests on over 300 campuses, created pro-war badges, bumper stickers (These stickers go on the back of your car to show your support.) and even mailed pro-war books and leaflets to an estimated 80,000 interested students. In 1968, the President of the committee Thompson urged fellow activists to: 'try to prove to President Nixon that victory is the only acceptable way to end the conflict.'

In a 1968 Gallup Poll, 56% of Americans approved of the police handling of the Chicago Democratic convention. In 1969, Richard Nixon made a televised speech about the 'silent majority.' The people of the United States that clearly supported the war but were not taking to the streets to show support about it. This proved to be popular. The President received thousands of letters and telegrams and 77% of these supported his actions and the war.

In 1970, there was notable support and campaigning with white workers, which resulted in several clashes with construction workers known as 'Hard Hats' in New York.

May 13th, 1967 was the largest pro-war march in New York. It was known as 'We support our boys in Vietnam' or the Americanism Pageant. It lasted nine hours and even sent a letter of support to General Westmoreland stating:

'The real heart of America is behind you all the way, and it's time it showed its true colors to the world.'

Parades like this were repeated on a smaller scale throughout the United States. In 1973, a large welcome home parade was organised in 1973.

There were other significant forms of protest and in 1970, the Pro-War group VIVA, Voices in Vital America, started to produce bracelets in support of bringing back Prisoners of War, P.O.Ws) They sold between 5-10 million bracelets, at between $2-$3 from 1970-1976 as well as other groups selling 50 million pro-war bumper stickers. This would provide huge funds to the pro-war groups.

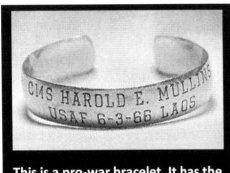

This is a pro-war bracelet. It has the name of the Missing soldier. It's aim was to bring to attention the soldier, the war, and support for the soldiers in general, as well as raise money to help get these troops back to America.

Here are some of the slogans that could be seen at the Pro-Vietnam War protests:

Bomb Berkley

Referring to the University in California.

Cong burn better than Flags

End the war in 1 day with 1 A bomb

This refers to the dropping of a nuclear bomb, which had been seriously discussed by General Westmoreland.

Bomb Hanoi Now

Referring to the North Vietnam Capital.

How do these compare with the anti-war slogans that you saw earlier?

These were televised committee meetings held by the United States Congress inside the Senate, from 1966 – 1971. Congress and the Senate are the equivalents of the British Parliament. The Chairman/leader of the hearings was called Fulbright, thus the name. Fulbright had been a Senator since 1945 and had been against the War and American involvement in other countries since taking office and had been opposed to the Vietnam conflict since the early 1960s. In 1966, he released the book, 'The arrogance of power' which criticised the American government for its involvement in Vietnam.

Fulbright had supported the Gulf of Tonkin resolution and some have argued his support was key for the resolution passing. However, soon after the passing new information began to surface about whether the event had taken place. Fulbright is quoted to have said:

"I felt that I had been taken…They weren't trying to stop the war at all; they were trying to win it. What his motives were and what moved him to pursue that policy has always been a mystery to me. I tried what best I could to persuade him not to."

Fulbright started the hearings to attempt to make the discussion public and President Johnson was angry.

Fulbright opened the hearings with this statement summarising their purpose:

"Under our system, Congress, and especially the Senate, shares responsibility with the President for making our Nation's foreign policy. This war, however, started and continues as a Presidential war in which the Congress, since the fraudulent Gulf of Tonkin episode, has not played a significant role. [...] The purpose of these hearings is to develop the best advice and greater public understanding of the policy alternatives available and positive congressional action to end American participation in the war."

This was televised and had anti-war protesters and pro-war protesters speaking about and debated the situation in Vietnam.

There were veterans of the Vietnam War and they spoke about their experiences of the Vietnam War. The testimonies of these veterans were in detail and explained how the Vietnamese had been mistreated, how the tactics had failed, and it proved to the American people that the war could not be won. The most important points to take away were that the war could not be won, that the committee hearings were televised and therefore brought into people's homes, and that Congress stopped the funding for the Vietnam War.

The hearing did bring the Vietnam War and Gulf of Tonkin incident to public attention and gave a platform to Vietnam veterans to be heard. In the short term, this did not stop the war, and by 1966 there were 400,000 American troops in Vietnam. However, by August 1967 the War was now being discussed in less than favourable terms.

As ever in history, the effects, significance and impact can be blurry.

Bibliography:

- ✓ The Pentagon Papers, Gravel Edition, (Boston: Beacon Press, 1971) Volume 1.
- ✓ *Vietnam: a History,* (Viking,1983) Stanley Karnow
- ✓ *Vietnam: An Epic Tragedy, 1945-1975, 1st Edition (Harper, 2018) Max Hastings*
- ✓ *Tonkin Gulf and the escalation of the Vietnam War, 1st Edition (University of North Carolina Press, 1996) Edwin Moise*
- ✓ *The Pro-War Movement: Domestic Support for the Vietnam War and the Making of Modern American Conservatism (Culture, Politics, and the Cold War) 1st Edition (University of Massachusetts Press, 2013) Sandra Scanlon*
- ✓ *The Vietnam War: An Intimate History (Knopf, 2017) by Ken Burns, Lynn Novick and Geoffrey Ward.*

Changing Nature of Warfare, 1918 - 2011

Complete Student Book: Full of Maps and Facts

Changing Nature of Warfare, 1918 - 2011,

Supplement Work Book: Full of Questions, Exam Technique and Tips.

Changing Nature of Warfare, 1918 - 2011,

Express Revision Work Book: Full of Questions, Exam Technique and Tips.

Where should I stay in Sicily? Ortigia & Syracuse/Siracusa

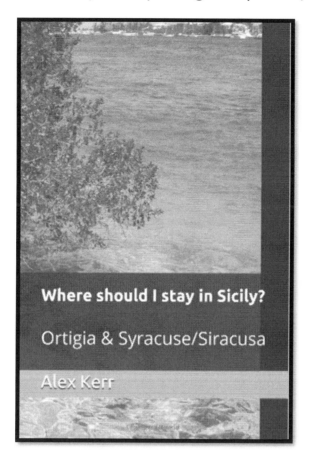

Printed in Great Britain
by Amazon